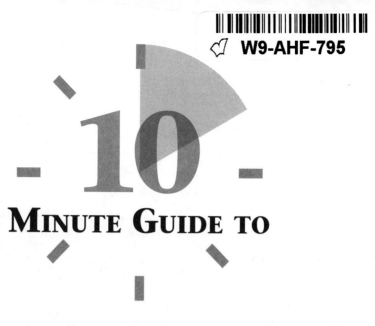

10 Minute Guide to

Schedule+ for Windows 95

by Sherry Kinkoph

A Division of Macmillan Computer Publishing
201 West 103rd St., Indianapolis, Indiana 46290 USA

To Jeff and Patti Crabtree and clan.

Special thanks to Martha O'Sullivan, Melanie Palaisa, and Rebecca Mayfield for assisting in the creation of this book.

International Standard Book Number: 0-7897-0568-0

Library of Congress Catalog Card Number: 95-71449

98 97 96 95   8 7 6 5 4 3 2 1

Interpretation of the printing code: the rightmost double-digit number is the year of the book's first printing; the rightmost single-digit number is the number of the book's printing. For example, a printing code of 95-1 shows that this copy of the book was printed during the first printing of the book in 1995.

Publisher Roland Elgey

Vice-President and Publisher Marie Butler-Knight

Publishing Manager Barry Pruett

Editorial Services Director Elizabeth Keaffaber

Managing Editor Michael Cunningham

Development Editor Melanie Palaisa

Production Editor Rebecca Mayfield

Designer Kim Scott

Cover Designer Scott Cook

Technical Specialist Cari Skaggs

Indexer Carol Sheehan

Production Team Anne Dickerson, Bryan Flores, DiMonique Ford, Julie Quinn, Karen L. York

Special thanks to Marty Wyatt for ensuring the technical accuracy of this book.

CONTENTS

INTRODUCTION

How did we ever keep organized before the advent of paper? Did the busy Cro-Magnon executive chisel his weekly appointments onto stone, or did he rely on leafy Post-It style notes stuck up with tar around the office cave? Over the years, we've evolved to rely on paper to organize our lives. (Of course, there are some gifted people who keep themselves organized without paper, but they're very rare.)

Paper helps us keep track of our busy lives. We remind ourselves of important meetings and dates with lists and notes scribbled onto large and small bits of paper or collections of paper. Organizing those many scraps of paper can often prove daunting. There are a variety of methods to employ, and perhaps you yourself use a combination of several. Some people file notes away into leather-bound organizers that they tote around everywhere they go; others keep their important papers in boxes that they hide in closets or push under the desk. Still others maintain their busy schedules through a visual display of sticky notes plastered about their desk and computer.

Regardless of your method of organization, there's plenty of room for disaster to strike. Nothing brings on a panic attack faster than realizing that you misplaced a piece of paper with crucial information on it. Suddenly, your organized life is in chaos.

Isn't it about time you evolved to use another organizational method, one without so much focus on paper? If you just purchased a copy of Microsoft's Schedule+ program, you're well on your way to evolving.

What Is Schedule+?

You can now organize yourself safely and electronically on your own computer with Microsoft's Schedule+. Schedule+ is actually a *Personal Information Manager*, or PIM, application. PIMs help you keep your daily life organized and free from unexpected chaos.

Schedule+ resembles a personal organizer, a time-management tool popular these days in the business community. Most organizers are set up with sections that you arrange in a three-ring binder. Each section in the binder helps you organize a particular part of your daily life. Schedule+ comes with sections, too. Here's what you'll find in your Schedule+ program:

- Appointment Book   Use this feature to keep track of daily and weekly appointments and to set up reminders. You can even set up alarms that beep to remind you of an appointment.

- To Do list   Organize your daily or weekly tasks and prioritize things you have to keep track of.

- Contacts   Enter your business contacts and keep a list of names, addresses, and phone numbers of people you need to reach often.

- Planner   Organize meetings and attendees with the Schedule+ Planner feature. The Planner's Meeting Wizard helps you coordinate meeting times.

- Events   Stay ahead of special occasions, including birthdays, anniversaries, conferences, and more, with the Events feature.

With Schedule+ you can keep track of daily appointments and meetings, prioritize your work, and do a whole lot more. Naturally, all of this electronic organization makes your life easier. At least you won't have to worry about losing bits of paper anymore, or trying to remember what you need to accomplish each day.

WELCOME TO THE *10 Minute Guide to Schedule+ for Windows 95*

Computer programs aren't always easy to wade through. There's a lot you need to know in order to make a program do what you want it to do. That's where this book helps. The *10 Minute Guide to Schedule+ for Windows 95* gives you straightforward, easy-to-understand lessons about using Schedule+ to accomplish specific tasks. This book gives you the information you need without all the technical jargon. Plus, you'll be able to complete each lesson in 10 minutes or less.

The *10 Minute Guide to Schedule+ for Windows 95* is for anyone interested in:

- Fast and easy information about setting up a daily schedule using a computer.

- Tips and steps for viewing a schedule by week or by month.

- Creating a comprehensive database of contacts.

- Learning about prioritizing tasks and projects.

- Using Schedule+ on a network to coordinate meetings with others.

HOW TO USE THIS BOOK

Each of the lessons in this book includes step-by-step instructions for using the Schedule+ program. You can read the book from start to finish, or you can pick and choose the lessons focusing on the tasks you want to learn. The first few lessons start with such tasks as opening and closing the Schedule+ program. Lesson-by-lesson, you progress to using Schedule+ to help you organize appointments, lists, and more. You even find lessons about using Schedule+ in a network environment.

If you're completely new to the Windows 95 environment, you might want to start with the "Windows 95 Primer" at the back of this book. If you're an experienced user and you need to get up and running with Schedule+ quickly, turn to Lesson 1 and start organizing your daily life now.

Conventions Used in This Book

Throughout this book are icons that identify tips to help you save time and learn important information fast.

Timesaver Tip icons mark tips that give you inside hints for using Schedule+ more efficiently.

Plain English icons identify definitions of new terms for you.

Panic Button icons alert you to warnings and cautions about potential problem areas.

You also find these conventions throughout the steps in the lessons:

What you type	Things that you type in appear in bold, color type.
Press Enter	Any keys that you press or items that you select with your mouse appear in color type.
On-screen text	Any messages that you see on-screen appear in bold type.

TRADEMARKS

All terms mentioned in this book that are known to be trademarks or service marks are listed below. In addition, terms suspected of being trademarks or service marks have been appropriately capitalized. Que Corporation cannot attest to the accuracy of this information. Use of a term in this book should not be regarded as affecting the validity of any trademark or service mark.

Schedule+ is a registered trademark of Microsoft Corporation.

STARTING AND EXITING SCHEDULE+

In this lesson, you will learn how to start, log on to, and exit Schedule+. You also learn how to change your logon password.

STARTING SCHEDULE+

To begin working with Schedule+, you first have to start the program. To start Schedule+, follow these steps:

1. Open the Start menu from the Windows 95 taskbar by clicking on the Start button.

2. From the Start menu, click on Programs.

3. In the Programs menu, select Microsoft Schedule+ to open the application (Figure 1.1).

TIP **Other Ways to Open Schedule+**   You can also launch Schedule+ from the Windows Explorer by double-clicking on the Schedule+ executable file in the Schedule+ folder. Or open Schedule+ from the My Computer window by opening the drive and folder containing the program and double-clicking on the Schedule+ icon.

LOGGING ON WITH THE LOGON BOX

The first thing you see when you start Schedule+ is a logon box. You see a logon box every time you open Schedule+. Depending on whether or not you are on a network (connected to other computers), your computer may show different logon boxes. If you're networked (and you share e-mail on the network with other users), you use a *group-enabled mode* box. If you're not connected to a computer network, you use a *stand-alone mode* box as shown in Figure 1.2.

Using Group-Enabled Mode The first time you open Schedule+, you have the option of using the program in group-enabled or stand-alone mode. If you're using Schedule+ on a network, be sure to select group-enabled mode. If you select the Don't ask me this question again check box, you won't be able to switch to another mode unless you reinstall Schedule+.

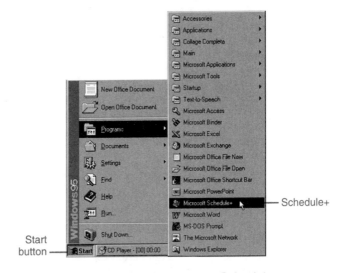

FIGURE 1.1   Use the Start button to open Schedule+.

FIGURE 1.2   The Schedule+ Logon dialog box.

Why go to the trouble of using a logon box? Because the things you keep in your Schedule+ program may be personal or private, and you may not want everyone to have access to your schedule. Logon names and passwords help you keep your data safe. Logon boxes are also useful if several people use the same computer. For example, if you use Schedule+ at home, other members of your family can set up and open their own schedules through the logon box.

Here are instructions for handling the logon modes:

- In group-enabled mode, type your name in the Profile name text box, type in your password (if assigned one), and click OK.

- In stand-alone mode, type your name in the User name text box, type in your password (if assigned one), and click OK.

If you logged onto Schedule+ previously and created a schedule, the logon box may already display your user name when you log on again.

The first time you create a schedule, the Schedule+ welcome box appears, as shown in Figure 1.3. (This box also appears when the program cannot find a schedule you previously created.)

FIGURE 1.3   The welcome box has two options you can choose.

- To create a new schedule, select the I want to create a new schedule file option and click OK.

- To open a schedule, select the I want to use an existing schedule file option and click OK

Either method opens the Select Local Schedule dialog box, shown in Figure 1.4. You use this dialog box to locate schedules or to simply confirm information about your new schedule, such as its name and location.

Use this drop-down list to save your schedule in another folder.

Schedule+ files use a .SCD filename extension.

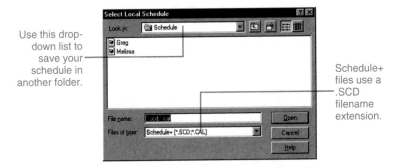

FIGURE 1.4   The Select Local Schedule dialog box.

- To confirm information about a new schedule, click on the Save button. If you want to save the schedule in another location, select a folder from the Save in drop-down list.

- To look for an existing schedule, use the Save in drop-down list to locate the folder containing the schedule. Once you find the schedule, select it and click on the Open button.

How Do I Start a New Schedule? If you share your computer with other people, such as family members, you probably want to know how to start new schedules for each user. To start a new schedule, you type a new logon name in the Schedule+ Logon dialog box. This sets up a schedule for the additional user that he or she can personally fill in.

Once you make it past the logon box and the startup procedure, your personal Schedule+ screen appears in full as shown in Figure 1.5.

The Schedule+ screen contains all the familiar Windows elements you've worked with before in other Windows programs. (You'll learn all about the parts of the Schedule+ screen in the next lesson.)

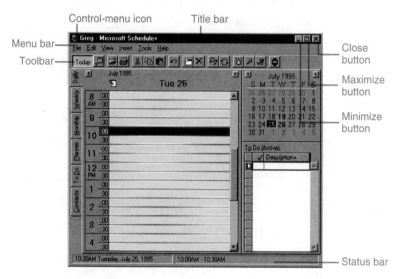

FIGURE 1.5 Welcome to Schedule+.

SETTING UP PASSWORDS

Passwords are a common feature of many computers and computer programs today. They help keep your data safe by only allowing users who know the password to access your files. You can set up a password for everyone who uses the Schedule+ program. If you use Schedule+ in a network environment, your network administrator may have already assigned you a password; however, you can change your password at any time.

To create or change a password for your Schedule+ program, perform the following steps:

1. Open the Tools menu and select Change Password.

2. In the Change Password dialog box, shown in Figure 1.6, type in a password.

3. Confirm the password by retyping it in the Verify new password text box.

4. Click OK. Schedule+ sets up the program with your new password.

You have to use the new password to log back onto the Schedule+ program. Be sure to remember your password, or write it down and keep it somewhere safe.

FIGURE 1.6   The Change Password dialog box.

EXITING SCHEDULE+

Although you're not ready to quit Schedule+ yet, you might as well learn how to exit it so you're ready when the time comes. To exit Schedule+, you can use any of these methods:

- Open the File menu and select Exit.
- Click on the Close button.
- Double-click on the program's Control-menu icon.
- Press Alt+F4.

Unlike many other programs you use, you don't have to take steps to save your data with Schedule+. It automatically saves your data when you exit the program.

In this lesson, you learned how to start Schedule+, to use the logon box and set your password, and to exit the program. In the next lesson, you'll learn how to navigate the Schedule+ screen.

NAVIGATING THE SCHEDULE+ SCREEN

In this lesson, you will learn how to move around and use the on-screen elements in Schedule+.

LOOKING AROUND THE SCHEDULE+ SCREEN

The whole Schedule+ program (see Figure 2.1) resembles one of those fancy personal organizer/planner books you buy at office stores, complete with tabs to separate your data. However, the pages of your organizer aren't held together by an expensive leather binder, and you don't have to lug it around with you. This organizer is all electronic, simple to use, and right by your side when you work on your computer.

The Schedule+ screen contains the same Windows 95 elements you use in other Windows 95 programs. Menus, toolbars, and scroll bars are in the familiar locations. But the Schedule+ program window looks a lot different from those of the other programs you use. For starters, there's a daily schedule (Appointment Book) on the screen, accompanied by a monthly calendar (Date Navigator) and a To Do list.

TIP

New to Windows 95? If you're new to the Windows 95 environment, you may want to browse the "Windows 95 Primer" at the back of this book. If you find you need more guidance than the primer offers, you might want to try the *10 Minute Guide to Windows 95* by Trudi Reisner to get up and running quickly.

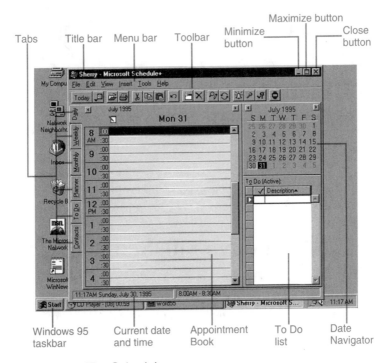

FIGURE 2.1   The Schedule+ screen.

Here's a description of each of the on-screen elements:

- **Title bar**   Notice that the title bar displays your name. That's because it's your schedule. If someone else starts a schedule on your computer, she sees her name on the title bar when she logs on.

- **Minimize, Maximize, and Close buttons**   Use these buttons to control the size of the program window.

- **Menu bar**   You find all of your Schedule+ commands on the various menus on the menu bar. To open a menu, simply click on its name.

- **Toolbar**   A faster way to activate commands and tasks is to click on the corresponding toolbar buttons. Each button on the toolbar controls a specific task or command.

To activate a button, click on it with your mouse pointer. (You learn more about the toolbar later in this lesson.)

- **Windows 95 taskbar** This is the bar at the bottom of your Windows 95 desktop (not part of the Schedule+ program). With Windows 95, you can have several programs open at once, and Windows 95 represents each open program with a button on the taskbar. Anytime you minimize a program, it reduces to a button on the taskbar.

- **Tabs** The left side of your Schedule+ window holds vertical tabs. Each tab represents a different feature of the program. For example, the Daily view tab enables you to view your Appointment Book in daily view. To view a different tab on your screen, click on the tab name.

- **Appointment Book** Use the Appointment Book to keep track of your daily schedule. You learn more about this feature in Lessons 4 and 5.

- **Date Navigator** To see the page for another date in the Appointment Book, you click on the date in the Date Navigator monthly calendar.

- **To Do list** Use this area to help you keep track of daily tasks you have to complete. (See Lesson 10 for more information.)

 What Day Is It? If you suddenly forget what day it is, look at your Schedule+ status bar for help. It always displays the current date and time.

You can use the mouse to move around the Schedule+ screen and select items, or you can use the keyboard shortcut keys and selection keys. Many of the on-screen items you work with have shortcut menus for accessing commands quickly. (You can right-click on an item to display a shortcut menu, when applicable.) For more information about using the mouse or keyboard to select on-screen items, or for more information about working with menus and dialog boxes, turn to the "Windows 95 Primer" in the back of this book.

When you first start Schedule+ you may notice that it doesn't make full use of your whole monitor screen (see Figure 2.1). You can use the program window control buttons to change how your Schedule+ window appears.

- If you prefer Schedule+ to fill your screen, simply click on the Maximize button.

- To return a maximized program window to its original size, click on the Restore button. (When you maximize a program, the Restore button appears so you can return the window to its previous size.)

- If you want to keep Schedule+ running but you want to move it out of the way while you work on other programs, minimize the program window to a button on the Windows 95 taskbar. Click on the Minimize button to do so.

- If you minimize Schedule+, you can open it again by simply clicking on its button on the taskbar.

WORKING WITH SCHEDULE+ TABS

There are six tabs along the left side of your screen. Each of these tabs enables you to use and view a specific Schedule+ feature. By default, Schedule+ is set up to open to the Daily view tab so that you can see the day's schedule of activities. However, you can open any tab by simply clicking on its name.

Here's a description of each tab and the feature it displays:

- **Daily** Click on this tab to view your daily schedule. You can quickly see your appointments and meetings arranged by times.

- **Weekly** Use the Weekly tab to view several consecutive days of your schedule at a glance.

- **Monthly**   To see your schedule for an entire month, like a calendar, click on the Monthly tab. As you can see in Figure 2.2, this view enables you to see several weeks of your schedule at a time.

These six tabs open specific Schedule+ features.

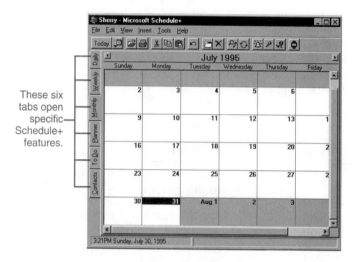

FIGURE 2.2   The Monthly view tab.

- **Planner**   To see your schedule in blocks of busy and free times, use the Planner view. With this view, you can also see the time blocks of other users on your network. See Lessons 16 and 17 for more on using Schedule+ on a network.

- **To Do**   Use this view to track and manage the tasks and projects that go along with your schedule. You can include a note to pick up the dry cleaning, you can write a grocery list, or you can list the complex project steps you must complete at work.

- **Contacts**   With Schedule+, you can compile a database of people you contact the most. You can keep an address book of clients, friends, and family that includes names, addresses, phone numbers, and more.

You'll learn more about each of these tabs in the lessons to come.

USING THE SCHEDULE+ TOOLBAR

The toolbar enables you to use shortcuts to common tasks such as printing or copying. To use the toolbar tools, click on the button you want to activate. Many of these buttons, such as Cut, Copy, and Paste, are the same as those in other Microsoft programs. However, there are plenty of new buttons on the toolbar as well.

Use this table to learn what each toolbar button does. (You'll learn more about these commands as we cover them in later lessons, but use this table as a reference.)

TABLE 2.1 SCHEDULE+'S TOOLBAR BUTTONS

BUTTON	NAME	DESCRIPTION
Today	Today	Opens your Appointment Book to the current date's schedule.
	Go To Date	Enables you to open your Appointment Book to a specific date.
	Open	Opens another person's schedule file.
	Print	Opens the Print dialog box so you can select portions of your schedule to print out.
	Cut	Cuts the data you selected and places it on the Windows Clipboard.
	Copy	Copies the data you selected and places the copy on the Windows Clipboard.
	Paste	Pastes data from the Windows Clipboard into your schedule at the insertion point.

BUTTON	NAME	DESCRIPTION
	Undo	Undoes your last action.
	Insert New Appointment	Opens a dialog box so you can insert an appointment into your schedule.
	Delete	Enables you to delete an appointment or task from your schedule.
	Edit	Opens a dialog box so you can edit appointments.
	Recurring	Helps you set up an appointment as a recurring event on your schedule.
	Reminder	Adds a reminder icon to your appointment or task.
	Private	Adds a private icon to your appointment or task.
	Tentative	Schedules the appointment as a tentative item on your schedule.
	Meeting Wizard	Leads you through the necessary steps for scheduling meetings on a network. (This button is only available in group-enabled mode.)
	Timex Watch Wizard	Enables you to upload schedule information onto your Timex Data Link watch.
	View Mail	Enables you to view your e-mail on the network mail system. (This button is only available in group-enabled mode.)

USING TOOLTIPS

If you ever have any doubt about what a toolbar button does, you can always find out by moving your mouse pointer over the button, pausing while the mouse pointer touches the button, and reading the ToolTip name that appears. If you don't see the ToolTip name, you may not have this feature turned on. To turn it on, follow these steps:

1. Open the Tools menu and select Options.

2. In the Options dialog box that appears (see Figure 2.3), click on the Display tab to bring this tab to the front of the dialog box.

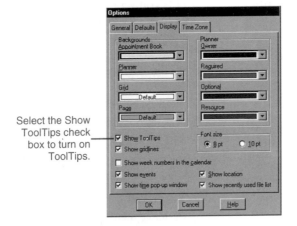

Select the Show ToolTips check box to turn on ToolTips.

FIGURE 2.3   The Options dialog box.

3. Select the Show ToolTips check box. A check mark in the check box means the ToolTips feature is on. (To turn it off, deselect the check box.)

4. Click OK to exit the Options dialog box.

In this lesson, you learned about the different elements of the Schedule+ screen and how to use the toolbar buttons. In the next lesson, you'll learn how to find online help.

GETTING HELP

In this lesson, you will learn how to access Help to get answers to your questions about Schedule+.

WORKING WITH THE HELP SYSTEM

If you ever get in a jam, you can call for help without dialing 911 by using Schedule+'s Help system. Help is an online system that assists you in times of trouble. Every Microsoft program has a Help menu on its menu bar. The Help menu offers several choices for looking up various topics with which you need assistance.

To display the Help menu, click on the word Help on the menu bar. This action opens the Help menu, which is shown in Figure 3.1.

FIGURE 3.1 The Help menu.

The Help menu has several options to choose from:

- **Microsoft Schedule+ Help Topics** Opens a dialog box of Help topics.

- **Answer Wizard** Opens a dialog box where you can type in a specific question, which the Answer Wizard then answers. Learn more about this unique feature later in this lesson.

- **Seven Habits Help Topics** Schedule+ comes with helpful information from the book *The Seven Habits of Highly Effective People.* You learn more about this information in Lesson 23.

- **The Microsoft Network** If your computer has a modem, and you have an account with the Microsoft Network online service, you can use this feature to help you connect to the network. Once you connect, you can access online help forums to assist you with any problems.

- **About Microsoft Schedule+** Opens a window containing information about the program version and maker.

What's a Wizard? Microsoft calls many of its automated features *wizards*. In short, a wizard is a step-by-step guide that leads you through a task or problem. When you select a wizard feature, such as the Answer Wizard, on-screen prompts appear asking you to choose from a variety of options.

USING THE HELP TOPICS DIALOG BOX

One way to access online Help is to use the Help Topics dialog box, shown in Figure 3.2. Within the dialog box are tabs with options for looking up online Help topics.

To open the Help Topics dialog box, follow these steps:

1. Open the Help menu and select Microsoft Schedule+ Help Topics.

2. The Help Topics dialog box opens, revealing its help options. To bring any tab to the front of the box, simply click on the tab name.

Exiting Dialog Boxes You can exit a dialog box at any time with any of these methods: click on the Close button in the upper-right corner of the dialog box; click on the dialog box's Cancel button; or press the Esc key.

Use the Contents tab to look up topics.

Use the Index tab to look up specific terms.

Use the Find tab to search for information.

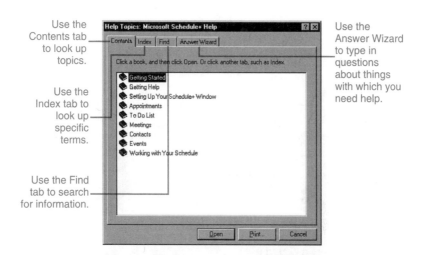

Use the Answer Wizard to type in questions about things with which you need help.

FIGURE 3.2   Help is on its way with the online Help system.

USING THE CONTENTS TAB

Click on the Contents tab in the Help Topics dialog box to view a list of available help topics (see Figure 3.3). To choose a topic, just double-click on its name or icon. This reveals a sublist of more topics, or opens up a help window detailing the topic. If you double-click on a topic and a sublist opens, keep double-clicking on related topics until you find the exact topic about which you want to view information. Note the several different icons that appear in the lists:

- A closed book icon next to a topic means there's a more-detailed list to view.

- An opened book icon next to a topic means the sublist for the topic is already in view.

- A question mark icon next to a topic means there's de-tailed text to view about the topic.

When viewing Help information, you see some terms with an underline and others with a dotted underline. When you click on an underlined word or phrase, Schedule+ jumps to a related help topic. When you click on a dotted underlined word or phrase, Schedule+ reveals a definition of the term.

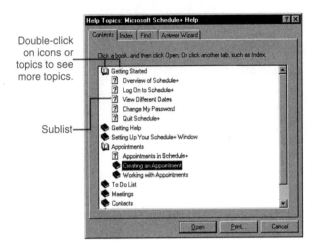

Double-click on icons or topics to see more topics.

Sublist

Figure 3.3   To select a topic from the list, double-click on a topic.

To use the Contents tab, follow these steps:

1. Double-click on the topic icon or topic phrase/word you want to view from the Contents list. (You can also select the topic and click on the Open button.)

2. If a sublist appears, double-click on the topic in the sublist that's related to the topic you want to view.

3. When you select a specific topic, Schedule+ displays the topic's Help window. The Help window reveals information pertaining to your topic, plus a menu bar and buttons. Figure 3.4 shows a Schedule+ Help window.

4. To close the Help window, click on the Close button.

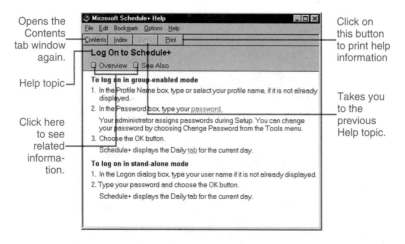

Opens the Contents tab window again.

Help topic

Click here to see related information.

Click on this button to print help information

Takes you to the previous Help topic.

FIGURE 3.4   Information about the selected topic appears in the window.

USING THE INDEX TAB

Click on the Index tab in the Help Topics dialog box to open another avenue for seeking help. The Index tab enables you to look up terms from a thorough index list (see Figure 3.5). Simply type in the word you want to look up, and the index scrolls alphabetically to the word or similar words in the list. From there you can double-click to display topics.

1. In the top text box in the Index tab, type in the first few letters of the word you want to look up.

2. The Index list box scrolls through the terms alphabetically the word you typed. When you see the entire word you want to look up in the list, just double-click on the word, or select the word and click on the Display button.

3. Information pertaining to the term appears in the Help window. To exit the Help window, click on the Close button.

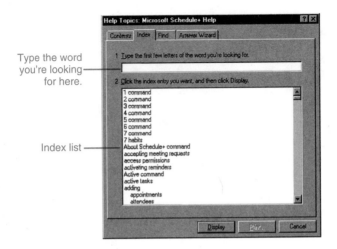

Type the word you're looking for here.

Index list

FIGURE 3.5   The Index tab.

LOOKING UP TOPICS WITH THE FIND TAB

Yet another way to look up Help topics is with the Find tab (see Figure 3.6), which is part of Microsoft's wizard collection. The Find tab helps you look up a specific topic based on words you type in. All the topics are in alphabetical order. You type in a word and use the drop-down list boxes to narrow your search.

To use the Find tab, follow these steps:

1. Type the word you're looking for in the step 1 text box. The drop-down lists in the step 2 and 3 boxes change to display words and topics related to what you type.

2. To narrow your search, select matching words from the step 2 list.

3. To select a word or phrase in the step 3 list box, click on the word or phrase and click on theDisplay button. This opens a window with information about the word or topic.

FIGURE 3.6   The Find tab.

USING THE ANSWER WIZARD

By far, the most innovative part of the Help system is the Answer Wizard. To open the Answer Wizard, you click on its tab in the Help Topics dialog box (which you open from the Help menu) or choose the Answer Wizard option directly from the Help menu. Figure 3.7 shows the Answer Wizard tab.

Inside the Answer Wizard tab, all you do is type in your request and click on the Search button, and the list box displays the answer. For example, if you're having trouble backing up a Schedule+ file, you can type in a question like "How do I backup a schedule?," and Answer Wizard answers you.

You can type in any kind of question, and Answer Wizard tries to respond to it. The Answer Wizard looks for key terms or words in the question and searches the online Help information for terms that meet the search criteria. Then the Answer Wizard supplies you with a list box of related topics, as shown in Figure 3.8. If you see something close to your request listed in the box, double-click on it to see detailed information about the subject matter.

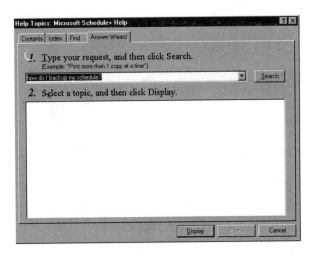

FIGURE 3.7 The Answer Wizard tab.

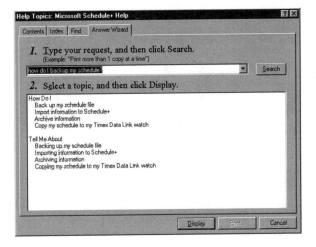

FIGURE 3.8 The Answer Wizard's answers.

To use the Answer Wizard, follow these steps:

1. Open the Answer Wizard tab. You can do this by opening the Help menu and selecting Answer Wizard. You can also select Microsoft Schedule+ Help Topics and select the Answer Wizard tab.

2. Type your question in the step 1 box and click on the Search button.

3. The results of the search appear in the step 2 box. To choose a topic, double-click on it.

4. To exit the dialog box, click on the Cancel button or the Close button.

OTHER HELP ROUTES

Aside from the Help menu and Help Topics dialog box, there are other ways to find help. Another way to get help is to press F1 on the keyboard. This opens the Help Topics dialog box directly. And speaking of dialog boxes, you can get help using them, too. Look for the help buttons (marked with a question mark icon) in the dialog boxes you work with to view more information about using the dialog box.

In this lesson, you learned how to access online Help. In the next lesson, you'll learn how to use the Daily view tab.

USING THE DAILY VIEW TAB

In this lesson, you will learn how to use the Daily view tab and work with its different features.

PARTS OF THE DAILY VIEW TAB

By default, Schedule+ always opens to the Daily view tab so you can see your day's appointments at a glance. Take a look at the Daily view tab in Figure 4.1.

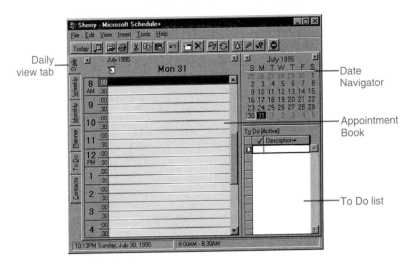

FIGURE 4.1 The Daily view tab.

There are several distinct parts of your Daily view tab. Three of them stand out in particular:

- The *Appointment Book* (the biggest part of your screen with all the times and lines in it) shows your daily schedule. You can use it to note appointments, meetings, and other items.

- Use the *Date Navigator* (the monthly calendar in the upper-right corner) to change the date in the Appointment Book.

- Use the *To Do list,* which appears right under the Date Navigator, to display a list of what you need to do on this date.

You can change the size of the display for the Appointment Book, Date Navigator, and To Do List by moving the lines that separate them. Follow these steps to resize the features:

1. Move your mouse pointer over any line between the Appointment Book, Date Navigator, or To Do list until the pointer becomes a double-headed arrow.

2. Hold down the left mouse button and drag the pointer to resize the screen items.

3. When the border reaches the desired new location, release the mouse button, and Schedule+ resizes the screen area.

CHANGING DATES IN THE APPOINTMENT BOOK

The Daily view tab always displays the current date on the Appointment Book when you first open Schedule+. To view other dates, you need to switch to other dates in your schedule. There are several ways to change the day that you view. Take a look at the Daily view tab screen again, shown in Figure 4.2.

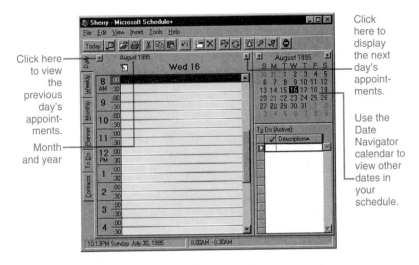

Click here to view the previous day's appointments.

Month and year

Click here to display the next day's appointments.

Use the Date Navigator calendar to view other dates in your schedule.

FIGURE 4.2   There are several ways to change the date you display in the Appointment Book.

Use the two tiny buttons with arrows on them (at the top of the Appointment Book area) to move backward and forward in your schedule as described here:

- A click on the left arrow button moves your schedule back one page to the previous date.

- A click on the right arrow button moves your schedule forward one page to the next date.

- Click on either the left or right arrow button and hold your mouse button down to speed through your schedule pages backward and forward, respectively.

 Back to Today   To quickly return to the current date, click on the Today button on the toolbar.

Another way to change dates quickly is to use the Date Navigator calendar. You simply click on a date on the calendar, and Schedule+ displays that date in the Appointment Book. Like the

Appointment Book area, the Date Navigator has two arrow buttons on the top of the calendar that enable you to view previous or future months.

- Click on the left arrow button to display the previous month.

- Click on the right arrow button to view the next month.

- To shuffle quickly through the months in either direction, position your mouse pointer so it touches the appropriate arrow and hold down the left mouse button. Let go of the mouse button when you reach the month you're looking for.

TIP   **Faster Calendar Selection**   You can also open a calendar quickly by clicking on the Go To Date button on the toolbar. When you click on this button, a calendar drops down, and you can select other dates to display.

CHANGING THE TIME DISPLAY

Not only can you change the days that you display in the Appointment Book, but you can also change the times. The scroll bar at the right of the Appointment Book enables you to scroll through the increments of time that appear in your daily schedule.

The Schedule+ program starts out with default settings for the time increments. The time frame the Appointment Book displays is set for typical use, and for most of us, this setting works just fine. For example, the Appointment Book typically shows an 8:00 a.m.—5:00 p.m. time frame broken down into 30-minute blocks in its window. However, you can always change this time frame to meet your own needs.

You change the time frame to suit the hours you keep using the Options dialog box. When you open this dialog box, you can use its four tabs to adjust settings for your schedule and screen display, and even to reset your time zone.

Follow these steps to change the Appointment Book's time display:

1. Open the Tools menu and select Options.

2. The Options dialog box appears on your screen. Click on the General tab to bring the time controls to the front of the dialog box (see Figure 4.3).

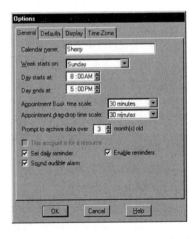

FIGURE 4.3   The General tab of the Options dialog box.

3. To change what time the day display begins, set a time in the Date starts at drop-down list by clicking the up or down spinner buttons, or by clicking in the text box and typing a new time.

4. To change what time the day display ends, set a time in the Day ends at drop-down list the same way you set the start time in step 3.

5. To change how the Appointment Book displays minute increments, open the Appointment Book time scale drop-down list and select a new increment.

6. Click OK to save your changes and exit the dialog box.

CHANGING THE TIME ZONE

You can also use the Options dialog box to change the Appointment Book's time zone. For example, you might find it useful to view your schedule in another time zone if you do business across the country or across the world. You can even display a secondary time zone to help you as you arrange appointments with colleagues in other time zones.

To change the time zone, follow these steps:

1. Open the Tools menu and select Options.

2. The Options dialog box appears on your screen. Click on the Time Zone tab to bring it to the front of the dialog box, as shown in Figure 4.4.

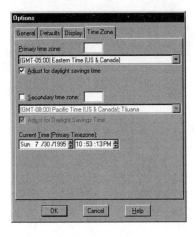

FIGURE 4.4   The Time Zone tab.

3. To change the time zone, click on the Primary time zone drop-down list and select a time zone for your

Appointment Book (see Figure 4.5). You can type a description for the time zone, like EST, in the text box next to the Primary time zone drop-down list. This information then appears on your daily schedule.

4. Click OK to close the box.

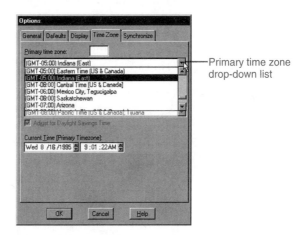

Primary time zone
drop-down list

Figure 4.5   Choose a new time zone from the Primary time zone drop-down list.

Changing the Appointment Book's Appearance

You can control how your Appointment Book looks with the Display tab in the Options dialog box, shown in Figure 4.6. You can change the background color of the daily schedule, and even change the point size of the text you use in the schedule.

Follow these steps to change the Appointment Book's appearance:

1. Open the Tools menu and select Options.

2. The Options dialog box appears on your screen. Click on the Display tab to bring this tab to the front of the dialog box.

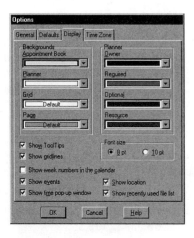

FIGURE 4.6   The Display tab.

3. To change the background, click on the Appointment Book drop-down list in the Backgrounds area and select a color.

4. To change font size for the appointment text (which you'll learn to enter in the next lesson), click on the Font size button you want to use.

5. Click OK to close the dialog box.

In this lesson, you learned about the various parts of the Daily view tab. In the next lesson, you'll learn how to set up appointments in the Appointment Book.

5

SCHEDULING APPOINTMENTS

In this lesson, you will learn how to set appointments in your daily schedule.

MAKING AN APPOINTMENT

Are you ready to start filling in your daily appointments? You can select any time slot in your Appointment Book and enter an appointment. Use the scroll arrows on the right side of the Appointment Book to move through your time schedule. (There are more hours than the typical 8:00 a.m.—5:00 p.m.; scroll up and down to find them.) Take a look at Figure 5.1.

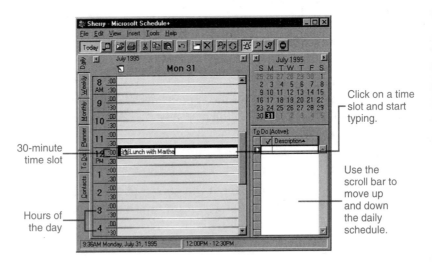

30-minute time slot

Click on a time slot and start typing.

Use the scroll bar to move up and down the daily schedule.

Hours of the day

FIGURE 5.1 Entering appointments is easy.

To enter an appointment, perform these steps:

1. Click on the time slot into which you want to insert the appointment.

2. Type in a description of the appointment. If you type an exceptionally long description, you may not be able to see the whole description in the Appointment Book's time slot.

3. When you finish, click anywhere outside of that time slot.

Your appointment is now set in the Appointment Book. How's that for fast? It's easier than actually writing in a paper appointment book. By default, Schedule+ assigns a reminder to the appointment; it appears as a bell icon at the front of the description. You'll learn more about reminders and other icons later in this lesson.

In many instances the appointments you're keeping track of require more time than 30 minutes. You can easily block out a longer time slot. To enter a longer appointment, follow these steps:

1. Click on the time slot where the appointment starts.

2. Hold down the left mouse button and drag to the ending time slot. This highlights all the slots you select, as shown in Figure 5.2.

3. Release the mouse button. You can now type in your appointment's description, and Schedule+ sets the appointment in your Appointment Book (see Figure 5.3).

My Life Is Longer Than 30-Minute Increments! If you prefer to work with increments of time other than the default 30-minute time slots, you can do so. Turn back to Lesson 4 and follow the steps for changing your Appointment Book's time increments.

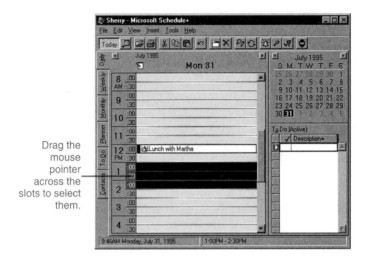

Drag the
mouse
pointer
across the
slots to select
them.

FIGURE 5.2   You can easily select more than one time slot when
you enter an appointment.

FIGURE 5.3   Here's an example of what a longer appointment
looks like in the Appointment Book.

Once you enter an appointment, you can do all sorts of things to it:

- You can edit the appointment at any time. (See Lesson 7.)
- You can move it to another date or copy it. (See Lesson 7.)
- You can delete it. (See Lesson 7.)
- You can view it in weekly or monthly view. (See Lesson 9.)
- You can set up the appointment so that Schedule+ reminds you when the appointment time gets close. (This feature is turned on by default.) More on this in Lesson 6.

You'll learn how to do each of these things in the lessons to come. In the meantime, there's another way you can enter appointments into your schedule.

 Quick Return to Today   You can return to the current **TIP**   date on your Appointment book by clicking on the Today button on your toolbar.

USING THE APPOINTMENT DIALOG BOX

Another route for entering more detailed appointments is to open the Appointment dialog box. To do this, double-click on a time slot. The Appointment dialog box appears on-screen, as shown in Figure 5.4. You can also access this dialog box by clicking on the Insert New Appointment button on the toolbar, or by opening the Insert menu and selecting Appointment.

The Appointment dialog box has four tabs for entering data. The General tab, shown in Figure 5.4, has options for setting up a new appointment. The following list explains what each one of these options controls:

Use these options to change times.

Use these options to change dates.

Type a description of your appointment here.

Select this option to set a reminder for your appointment.

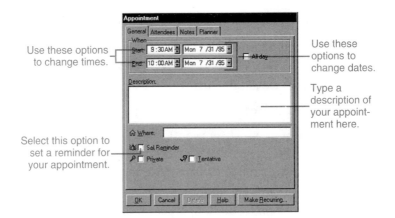

FIGURE 5.4   The Appointment dialog box.

- **When**   This area shows the start and end times of your appointment. You can type in other times and dates as needed. The arrow buttons next to the times enable you to scroll through other hours. The drop-down arrows next to the dates enable you to view a monthly calendar to select a new date.

- **Description text box**   This text box is where you type in details about your appointment. For example, let's say you're entering your lunch date with Bob in your daily schedule. You can type **Lunch with Bob** in the description text box. When you close the Appointment box, this description appears in your daily schedule.

- **Where**   You can type the location of the appointment in this text box.

- **Set Reminder**   If you want a reminder of your appointment beforehand (an on-screen message and an audible beep), select the Set Reminder option. When you select this option, additional controls appear for designating when the reminder message is to appear. (The message that appears is simply a dialog box telling you about your appointment.) For example, you can set it up to send you a reminder message fifteen minutes before your appointment. When you add a Reminder option to your appointment, a tiny bell icon appears next to the description in your schedule.

- **Private**   To keep your appointment descriptions away from the prying eyes of others, use the Private option. This hides your appointments from other users on your computer network, but you can still see the appointments in your schedule. When you add the Private option, a tiny key icon appears next to your appointment description.

- **Tentative**   If your appointment is tentative, use the Tentative option. This keeps the appointment time from appearing as untouchable in your Planner feature. This is beneficial if you're networked and people are trying to set up meetings with you. (More about the Planner in Lesson 15.) When you select the Tentative option, a tiny check mark with a question mark icon appears next to the description in your schedule.

- **Command buttons**   The command buttons at the bottom of the dialog box are standard. Use the Delete button to remove appointments, and use the Make Recurring button to set up an appointment as a regular recurring part of your schedule.

To set an appointment with the Appointment dialog box, follow these steps:

1. Double-click on any time slot in your daily schedule. This opens the Appointment dialog box.

2. Click on the General tab to bring its options to the front of the dialog box.

3. Set a specific time and date in the Start and End drop-down lists by clicking the up and down spinner buttons or clicking in the Start and End text boxes and typing a time and date. (By default, these boxes show the current

date and the time of the time slot you double-clicked on in your schedule.)

4. Type a description for your appointment in the Description text box.

5. You can add any additional options, such as a reminder or a recurring appointment, by selecting those options now.

6. When you finish, click OK, and Schedule+ sets your appointment. The appointment now appears on your schedule.

OPTION ICONS

When you assign an option such as a reminder to your appointment, an icon appears next to the description in your daily schedule. You need to learn to recognize the icons that appear in your Appointment Book and remember what they mean. Table 5.1 should help you out.

TABLE 5.1 THE APPOINTMENT BOOK'S OPTION ICONS

ICON	NAME	DESCRIPTION
🏠	Location	Indicates that there is a specific meeting place for the appointment.
🔔	Reminder	Schedule+ reminds you about the upcoming appointment as it gets closer.
🔑	Private	Schedule+ keeps other users on your network from seeing the appointment (if you're networked).
?	Tentative	Schedule+ notes the appointment as a tentative item on the schedule.

In Lesson 6, you'll find details about using each of these option icons in your own Appointment Book.

Use Your Toolbar, Too! You also find icons for the Reminder, Private, and Tentative options on the toolbar. When entering appointments directly without using the Appointment dialog box, click on the appropriate button on the toolbar to use any of these three options. You can turn the options on or off by clicking on the toolbar buttons.

USING THE OTHER APPOINTMENT DIALOG BOX TABS

There are some other things you can do in the Appointment dialog box besides set appointments. If you're networked, the other tabs in the Appointment box are useful for scheduling appointments.

- Use the Attendees tab to view a list of the people who are attending the appointment with you. (See Lesson 16 for more information.)

- Use the Notes tab to create notes about your meeting or to type up a meeting agenda to distribution to the attendees. (See Lesson 7 for an explanation about how to use the Notes tab.)

- Use the Planner tab, a miniaturized Planner feature that you'll learn about in Lesson 15, to view everyone's schedules to help you pick a free time for all. The Auto-Pick button helps you locate the first free time available for all of the attendees.

In this lesson, you learned how to add an appointment to your daily schedule. In the next lesson, you'll learn how to add the many appointment options to your appointments.

LESSON 6

SETTING UP APPOINTMENT OPTIONS

In this lesson, you will learn how to use the various appointment options to enhance your daily schedule.

SETTING A REMINDER

Do you have any pressing appointments that you can't possibly miss? Then the Reminder feature can really help you remember them. You already learned a little about inserting a reminder icon into your appointment in Lesson 5. When you set an appointment, a reminder icon that resembles a tiny bell appears in front of your appointment description, as shown in Figure 6.1.

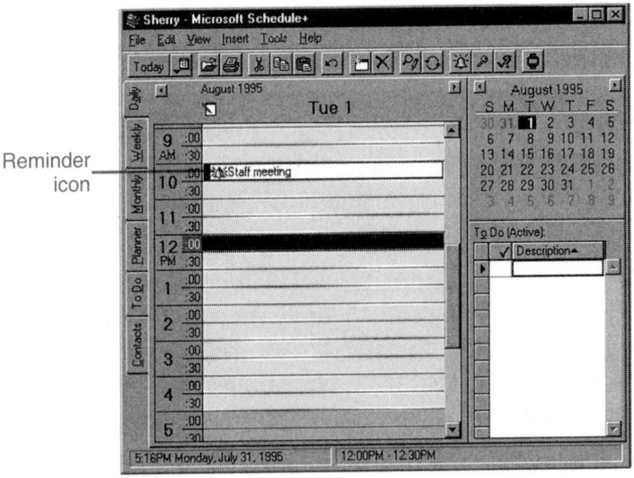

Reminder icon

FIGURE 6.1   Reminder icons are easy to spot in your daily schedule.

By default, Schedule+ inserts a reminder icon whenever you type a description in the daily schedule. You can also insert a reminder using the Appointment dialog box.

It Didn't Remind Me!   If you set a reminder for a time setting that's already passed, the reminder can't alert you to the appointment. For example, if it's 3:00 and you add a 3:15 appointment to your schedule with a 20-minute prior warning, you will not receive the reminder.

To set a reminder with the Appointment dialog box, follow these steps:

1. Double-click on the appointment in the Appointment Book, or click on the Insert New Appointment button on the toolbar to add a new appointment to your schedule.

2. The Appointment dialog box appears on-screen. Make sure you select the Set Reminder check box. When you select this option, additional options appear in the dialog box, as shown in Figure 6.2.

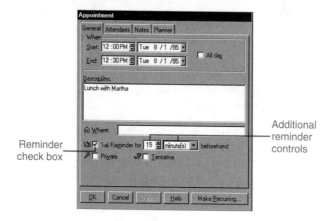

FIGURE 6.2   The Appointment dialog box.

3. Choose an advance time for the reminder to have Schedule+ display a reminder box on-screen when the appointment draws near.

4. To exit the dialog box, click OK.

Quick Reminders To quickly insert a reminder icon for an existing appointment, select the appointment and click on the Reminder button on the toolbar.

After setting a reminder, you will be reminded about your appointment only when it's time for the reminder to appear. (You learn all about the Reminder message box later in this section.) In order for the reminder to work, however, you must have your Schedule+ program open or minimized.

TURNING OFF THE DEFAULT REMINDER SETTING

If you get tired of Schedule+ inserting a reminder icon every time you type an appointment into the Appointment Book, you can turn off the default setting. To turn off reminders, follow these steps:

1. Open the Tools menu and select Options.

2. In the Options dialog box, click on the Defaults tab.

3. Deselect the Set reminders for appointments automatically check box.

4. Click OK to exit the Options dialog box.

To turn the default setting back on again, simply repeat the steps above, this time selecting the automatic reminder check box.

USING THE REMINDER MESSAGE BOX

But when does the Reminder feature get around to reminding you? It depends. What advance time did you set? You can control when the Reminder feature reminds you of an appointment.

In the Appointment dialog box, you can select the Set Reminder check box to choose what time the Reminder feature calls your attention to the appointment. Fifteen minutes beforehand is a typical setting.

The catch to using this feature, however, is that you need to have your computer on and have Schedule+ running (or minimized). In addition, you need to be in the same room with your computer or you won't see or hear the reminder.

When your appointment nears, the Reminder message box pops up on your screen (depending on when you set it to appear), as shown in Figure 6.3. When the Reminder message box appears, you hear an audible beep, and the message box suddenly interrupts what you are doing. The message box itself displays your appointment and its scheduled time.

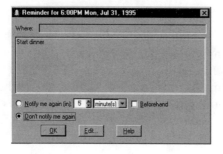

FIGURE 6.3   The Reminder box pops up on your screen to remind you about your appointment.

In the Reminder message box, you also see a description of the appointment and where your appointment is to take place (if you entered this information when you created the appointment). With the options at the bottom of the box, you can choose to remind yourself of the appointment again as the time for the appointment gets even closer.

- Click on the Notify me again option if you want another reminder before the appointment, and then select a time for the reminder.

- If you don't need another reminder, select the Don't notify me again option.

When you finish with the Reminder message box, click OK to exit.

I Didn't Get a Reminder!   By default, Schedule+ is set to show reminder boxes along with an audible beep. However, if you turned these settings off, you may be missing all of your reminder boxes. To check, open your Tools menu, select Options, and click on the General tab. Select the Set daily reminder, Set audible alarm, and Enable reminders check boxes. Click OK to exit, and your reminder boxes should work.

Setting Recurring Appointments

Some of your appointments happen every week or every day, such as a weekly staff meeting or a daily car pool. Rather than typing these appointments over and over again in your schedule, use the Recurring option. The Recurring option is available on your toolbar, in your Insert menu, and even in the Appointment dialog box. Here's one way to set up a recurring appointment:

1. Select the appointment on your schedule.

2. Click the Recurring button on your toolbar. This opens the Appointment Series dialog box. (See Figure 6.4.)

3. Use the tabs to set up information about your recurring appointment. Click on the When tab to designate when the appointment occurs (daily, weekly, monthly, or yearly) and what day it falls on. You can also set the exact time of the meeting. Make your adjustments to the settings.

4. To set a reminder for the appointment, click on the General tab, which looks just like the one in the Appointment dialog box. Use the Set Reminder option to add a reminder to the recurring appointment.

5. Click OK to exit the dialog box, and Schedule+ sets your recurring appointment.

A recurring appointment always appears with a circular icon beside it in your Appointment Book.

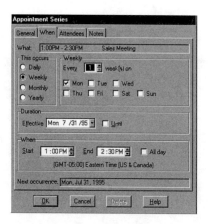

FIGURE 6.4   The Appointment Series dialog box.

SETTING PRIVATE AND TENTATIVE APPOINTMENTS

If you're using Schedule+ on a network, you'll be happy to know about the Private option. This option enables you to keep appointments hidden from others who have access to your schedule on the network. By assigning the Private icon to an appointment, you can keep others from viewing the details about the appointment. To assign a private icon to a selected appointment, simply click on the Private button on the toolbar.

Another way of keeping important items on your schedule away from prying eyes is to use the Hide Text command. After you assign a private icon to your appointment, follow these steps to hide the text:

1. Open the View menu and select Hide Private Text.

2. Click anywhere outside of the appointment, and Schedule+ hides the text description on your daily schedule. See Figure 6.5.

3. To see the text again, click inside the appointment or repeat step 1 to turn off the Hide Private Text view.

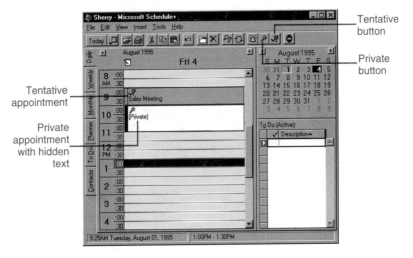

FIGURE 6.5 Here's an example of what a private icon and a tentative appointment look like.

The Tentative option enables you to set up a tentative appointment in your daily schedule. Schedule+ applies shading to tentative appointments (see Figure 6.5). This shading clearly lets you know that the time slot can be made available if more pressing engagements come up. To make an appointment tentative, click on the appointment slot that holds the appointment, and click on the Tentative button on the toolbar.

In this lesson, you learned how to add appointment options to your daily schedule. In the next lesson, you'll learn how to edit and move appointments in the Appointment Book.

JUGGLING APPOINTMENTS

In this lesson, you will learn how to edit and move your appointments.

EDITING APPOINTMENTS

In previous lessons, you learned how to enter appointments and add options to them. So, what if you want to change an appointment? In paper organizers, you can make changes to things you've written down by simply scribbling them out, or erasing and writing the appointments somewhere else in your schedule. In your electronic organizer, you can scribble things out too, but it works a little differently. And you don't have to worry about smudging your schedule or creating a giant ink blob on the screen.

There are several different ways to edit your scheduled appointments. You can use toolbar buttons or menu commands, or you can take a more direct approach. To make a change directly to an appointment in the Appointment Book, follow these steps:

1. Click inside the time slot to select it. You can double-click on the time slot to display a shortcut menu that contains related commands (see Figure 7.1).

2. You can edit the description text just like you edit text in a word processing program. You can delete characters, insert new words, and so on.

3. To turn appointment options on or off, simply click on the appropriate toolbar buttons. For example, to add a reminder to the appointment, click on the Reminder button.

4. When you finish editing, click anywhere outside the time slot.

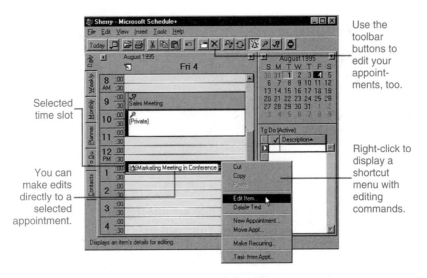

Selected
time slot

You can
make edits
directly to a
selected
appointment.

Use the
toolbar
buttons to
edit your
appoint-
ments, too.

Right-click to
display a
shortcut
menu with
editing
commands.

FIGURE 7.1   Editing is a breeze in Schedule+.

ADDING AND DELETING APPOINTMENTS

To add new appointments to your schedule, simply follow the
steps you learned in Lesson 5. You can add new appointments
directly onto your Appointment Book schedule, or your can add
them with the Appointment dialog box. To add a new appointment to your schedule with the Appointment dialog box, double-
click on the time slot where you want it to appear, or click on the
Insert New Appointment button on the toolbar. This opens the
Appointment dialog box that you fill in with details about the
appointment.

It's very easy to remove appointments from your schedule. There
are several procedures you can use. First, select the appointment
you want to delete; then follow any of these methods:

- Click on the Delete button on the toolbar.

- Double-click on the appointment to open the Appointment dialog box and click on the Delete button.

- Open the Edit menu and choose Delete Item.

- Press the Delete key on your keyboard.

- Right-click on the appointment to open a shortcut menu and select Delete Item.

CHANGING AN APPOINTMENT'S TIME

You can increase or decrease the time allotted for your appointment by dragging its border to a new beginning time or ending time. Use these steps to change the appointment's time:

1. Move your mouse pointer over the bottom border of the selected time slot. The mouse pointer becomes a double-headed arrow, as shown in Figure 7.2.

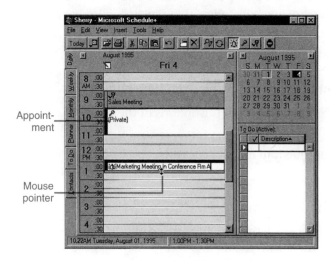

FIGURE 7.2   The first step in changing the time length is to move your mouse pointer over the border.

2. Hold down your left mouse button and drag the box to a new beginning or ending time.

3. Release the mouse button, and the appointment fills the new time slots.

I Can't Decrease My Appointment Beyond the Time Increment! If you have a short appointment that only lasts 15 minutes and your schedule is set up in 30-minute increments, you can't decrease the appointment to show less time than the time slot increments you set up. The 15-minute appointment fills up the whole 30-minute time slot.

MAKING CHANGES USING THE APPOINTMENT DIALOG BOX

Another route to editing appointments is to open and edit them in the Appointment dialog box. To edit an appointment using the Appointment dialog box, follow these steps:

1. Select the appointment in the Appointment Book and click on the Edit button on the toolbar (or double-click on the appointment's time slot). This opens the Appointment dialog box containing the appointment's details.

2. Make your changes to the options in the dialog box.

3. Click OK to exit the dialog box. Schedule+ changes the appointment to match your edits.

RESCHEDULING APPOINTMENTS

If you want to move the appointment to another time slot, you can drag it there with the mouse. Follow these steps to move an appointment in your daily schedule:

1. Position your mouse pointer over the left edge of the appointment that you want to relocate. The mouse pointer takes the shape of a four-headed arrow, as shown in Figure 7.3.

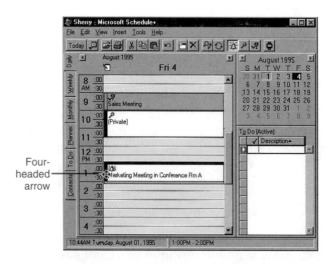

Four-headed arrow

FIGURE 7.3   Click on the left border to select the appointment for moving.

2. Hold down the left mouse button and drag the appointment to a new time slot. Notice that only the appointment's frame moves with the dragging motion (see Figure 7.4).

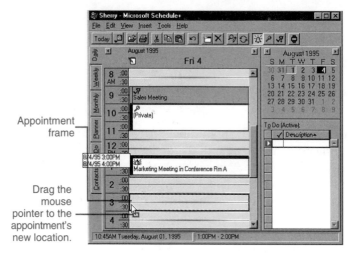

Appointment frame

Drag the mouse pointer to the appointment's new location.

FIGURE 7.4   Moving the appointment.

3. Release the mouse button, and Schedule+ moves the appointment.

MOVING APPOINTMENTS WITH THE MOVE APPOINTMENT DIALOG BOX

An even simpler way to move an appointment is with the Move Appointment dialog box. Use these steps to activate the dialog box:

1. Select the appointment you want to move.

2. Open the Edit menu and choose Move Appt.

3. When the Move Appointment dialog box appears, select a new time and date for the appointment. (See Figure 7.5.)

Choose a new time...   or choose a new date.

FIGURE 7.5   The Move Appointment dialog box.

4. Click OK to exit the dialog box. Schedule+ displays the appointment in its new date and time slot.

MOVING APPOINTMENTS WITH THE DATE NAVIGATOR

If you want to reschedule an appointment for a future date, use the Date Navigator (the calendar in the upper-right corner). As you may recall from Lesson 2, you can use the Date Navigator to view other dates in your schedule. When you click on the appropriate date on the calendar, your Appointment Book turns to that date's schedule page. The tiny arrow buttons at the top of the Date Navigator enable you to move back and forth between months so you can view and select other dates on your schedule.

The Date Navigator also comes in handy when you want to move an appointment to another date. To move an appointment with the help of the Date Navigator, use these steps:

1. In the Date Navigator calendar, locate the month and date to which you want to move an appointment. (Use the Date Navigator arrow buttons to display the correct month.)

2. In the Appointment Book, select the appointment you want to move.

3. Hold down the left mouse button and drag the appointment over to the Date Navigator calendar to the new date.

4. Let go of your mouse button, and Schedule+ moves the appointment to the other date's daily schedule.

CUT, COPY, AND PASTE

You can also use the Cut, Copy, and Paste commands to move your appointments. Schedule+ places cut or copied appointments in the Windows Clipboard, a temporary holding area. When you want to place the appointment in a new location, use the Paste command.

Follow these steps to use cut or copy and paste to move an appointment to a new location:

1. Select the appointment you wish to move or copy.

2. Click on the Cut or Copy button on the toolbar.

3. Move your schedule to the new date where you wish to place the appointment.

4. Click on the Paste button on the toolbar, and Schedule+ inserts the appointment in the new location.

ADDING NOTES TO APPOINTMENTS

With paper organizers, it's easy to add notes to your schedule: all you have to do is scribble your notes down. You can also add notes to your electronic schedule. You can create detailed notes along with any appointment you set. The notes don't appear in the daily schedule, but you can view your notes in the Appointment dialog box.

Follow these steps to add notes to an appointment:

1. Select the appointment to which you wish to add notes.

2. Click on the Edit button on the toolbar to open the Appointment dialog box.

3. Click on the Notes tab to bring this tab to the front of the dialog box.

4. In the empty text box that appears, you can type all kinds of notes or jot down your thoughts.

5. To exit the dialog box, click OK.

To see the notes regarding the appointment, double-click on the appointment to open the Appointment dialog box again and click on the Notes tab to read them.

In this lesson, you learned how to edit and move appointments in your daily schedule. In the next lesson, you'll learn how to add events to the Appointment Book.

ADDING EVENTS TO YOUR SCHEDULE

In this lesson, you will learn how to add, reschedule, and edit events in your schedule with the Event feature.

USING THE EVENT SCHEDULER

Need to schedule a big event or an annual event on your busy calendar? Use the Event Scheduler to help you. Events show up a little differently on your schedule than appointments do. Events appear at the top of your daily schedule, right under the day and date. Events do not affect your time slots. For example, if you set up the schedule to show a Sales Recognition Day as an event, it appears at the top of your schedule, as shown in Figure 8.1. (If you switch over to weekly view, which you'll learn about in Lesson 9, events appear at the top of the day of the week on which they occur.)

What constitutes a big event? I consider my vacation to be a very big event, so I'm always trying to work it into my busy schedule. Other events might include out-of-town conferences or conventions, weddings, training classes, seminars, company trips, birthdays, and more. Events can be a one-day thing, or they can span days, weeks, or even months. With Schedule+, you can set recurring events so that they show up each week, month, or year. Recurring events are called Annual Events in Schedule+.

Event —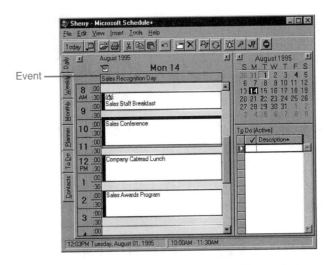

FIGURE 8.1   Schedule+ enables you to add events to your schedule.

Here's a list of events you may have a use for in your own schedule:

- Conferences and conventions
- Classes and seminars
- Vacations and holidays
- Birthdays
- Weddings and anniversaries
- Retirements
- Promotional events (such as End-of-Month Sale)
- Office events (such as Staff Recognition Day)

Birthday Events   Be sure to set up the birthdays of your friends and family members as events in your calendar. That way, you can spot them right away. If you set them up as recurring events, those birthdays appear on your schedule every year!

ADDING EVENTS

Here's what you do to add an event to your schedule:

1. Click on the Event icon at the top of your schedule, as shown in Figure 8.2.

Event icon

Event submenu

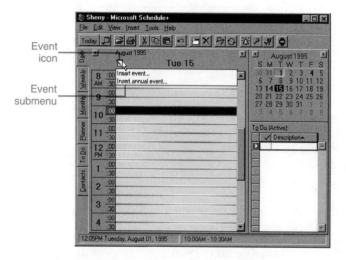

FIGURE 8.2   Add an event to your personal schedule with the Event feature.

2. When you click on the Event icon, a submenu appears (see Figure 8.2) with the options Insert event or Insert annual event. (If you select Insert annual event, you make the event a recurring part of your schedule.)

3. Choose Insert Event or Insert annual event for the event you want to add. Either the Event or Annual Event dialog box appears on your screen. Figure 8.3 shows the Event dialog box.

4. In the dialog box, choose the event start date. If you insert an event with the Event dialog box, you should also choose an end date. You can use the arrow buttons next to the dates to choose other dates, or you can type in the dates you want.

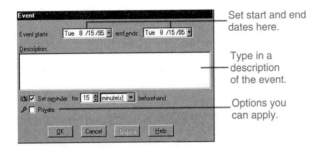

Set start and end dates here.

Type in a description of the event.

Options you can apply.

FIGURE 8.3   The Event dialog box.

Use the Menu Approach You can also open the Insert menu and select Event to open the Event dialog box. If you're setting an annual event, select Annual Event from the Insert menu to open the Annual Event dialog box.

5. Click in the Description text box and type in a description of the event.

6. Add any additional options, such as a reminder or a private icon.

7. Click OK to exit the dialog box. The event appears on your schedule as a heading at the top of the event day column, as shown in Figure 8.4.

When you set an event in your schedule, the Event icon looks like it has writing on it. That's one way you can tell you planned an event that day. An event day also appears in bold type on the Date Navigator calendar.

EDITING AND RESCHEDULING EVENTS

You can easily edit events at any time by reopening the Event or Annual Event dialog box and making your changes. To edit an event, follow these steps:

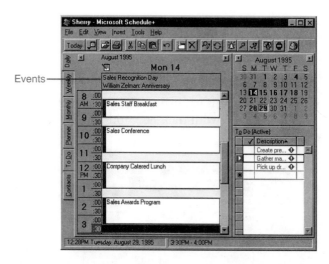

FIGURE 8.4   Here's an example of how events appear on your schedule.

1. Click on the Event icon. This time, your event's description appears in the submenu. You can also click directly on the Event description at the top of your daily schedule to view the submenu.

2. Double-click on the event's description in the submenu to open the Event or Annual Event dialog box.

3. Make your changes in the dialog box. For example, to change the description, edit the description text. To change any options, simply turn the option check boxes on or off.

4. Click OK to exit the dialog box.

LISTING EVENTS

Another way to edit your events or to see a list of events is to use the Edit menu. This is especially helpful when you want to edit events that do not appear on the current day in your schedule. To edit or list your events, use these steps:

1. Open the Edit menu and select Edit List of. Schedule+ displays a submenu.

2. From the submenu, select Events or Annual Events, depending on which type of event you want to edit.

3. An Events list box opens up, listing all of the events you have scheduled, along with their descriptions and start dates. (See Figure 8.5.)

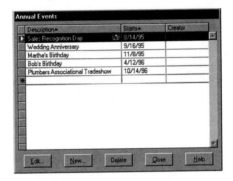

FIGURE 8.5   The Events list box.

4. To make changes to a specific event, select it and click on the Edit button. This opens the Event dialog box, shown previously in Figure 8.3. Make your edits to the event and click OK.

5. To add a new event to the list, click on the New button. This opens a new Event dialog box where you can enter detailed information about the event.

Delete It!   You can easily delete an event from the Events list by selecting it and clicking on the Delete button.

6. To exit the Events list box, click on the Close button.

To reschedule or move an event, you can open up the Events list box again and change the date by editing the event itself.

In this lesson, you learned how to add, reschedule, and edit events in your daily schedule. In the next lesson, you'll learn how to use the Weekly and Monthly view tabs.

USING THE WEEKLY AND MONTHLY TABS

In this lesson, you will learn how to view your schedule with the Weekly and Monthly tabs.

VIEWING APPOINTMENTS WITH THE WEEKLY TAB

It's time to switch views. How about looking at your busy schedule in a weekly format? You need to click on the Weekly tab. When you do this, your screen displays the Appointment Book in a slightly different view, as shown in Figure 9.1.

By default, Schedule+ shows you five days of the week in Weekly view. You no longer see the Date Navigator or the To Do list. Your screen looks a little crowded in Weekly view, and some of your appointments may not fit completely into your weekly columns. Don't forget, you can enlarge the Schedule+ screen by clicking on the Maximize button. (If your appointment text is too long to fit in Weekly view and you still can't see the full appointment text, switch back to Daily view to read it all.) You can also double-click on an appointment's border in Weekly view to open the Appointment dialog box and see details about the appointment.

The schedule you see in the Weekly view is the same as the schedule in Daily view; however, you see more days of the week in the Weekly view. You can perform the same functions in your Weekly view as in Daily view. The scroll bar at the far right side of the Weekly view screen enables you to scroll through the time slots on the schedule.

Left arrow button

Event

Weekly tab

Days

Right arrow button

Event icon

Appointments

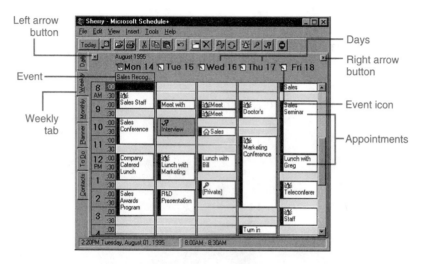

FIGURE 9.1   To change to the Weekly view, click on the Weekly tab.

CHANGING WEEKS

At the top of the Weekly view tab are two arrow buttons, shown in Figure 9.1, one on the left and one on the right. Like the arrow buttons in Daily view, you can use these arrow buttons to move your Weekly view back a week or forward a week.

To change weeks, use any of these methods:

- To move forward to the next week, click once on the right arrow button.

- To move back to the previous week, click once on the left arrow button.

- If you hold down your mouse button while selecting the appropriate arrow button, you move quickly forward or backward through the weeks of the month.

CHANGING THE DAY DISPLAY

You can easily change the number of days that Schedule+ displays in the Weekly view tab. To change the day display, follow these steps:

1. Open the View menu and select Number of Days (see Figure 9.2).

FIGURE 9.2   Use the View menu to change the day display. For example, to view all seven days of the week, choose 7 from the list.

2. In the submenu that appears, choose the number of days you want to display in the Weekly view tab. The Weekly view changes to reflect your selection, as shown in Figure 9.3.

SPECIFY YOUR WORKWEEK AND WORK HOURS

The General tab in the Options dialog box holds settings that affect when your schedule week starts, which days of the week are work days or non-work days, which hours are daily work hours and non-work hours, and what time increments are displayed, among other options. (You've already learned how to change the time increments back in Lesson 4.)

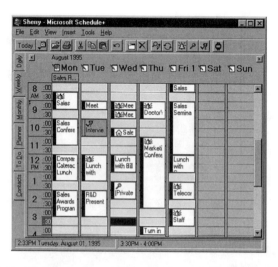

FIGURE 9.3   You can change the number of days Schedule+ displays by using the View menu.

The day your workweek starts affects the display of days in the Date Navigator calendar and the days of the week that show in the Weekly view tab. The workdays and hours also affect the background colors of your schedule. As you may notice, the workweek appears in a brighter shade of color on the schedule, and non-work days and non-work hours appear in a darker shade.

Not everybody uses the same workdays and work hours, so you can adjust these settings to help you tailor the program to your situation. To change the settings for workweeks and workdays, you use the Options dialog box. To change what day of the week your workweek starts on, and what work hours you want to focus on, follow these steps:

1. Open the Tools menu and select Options.

2. Click on the General tab in the Options dialog box to bring it to the front and locate the Week starts on option, as shown in Figure 9.4. To change the day, click on the arrow in the drop-down list and select the appropriate day to start your workweek.

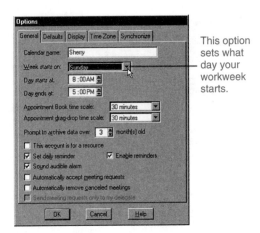

This option sets what day your workweek starts.

FIGURE 9.4   Click on the arrow to display a drop-down list of the days of the week.

3. To change the hours that you designate as your work hours and non-work hours, change the settings in the Day starts at and Day ends at boxes.

4. To exit the dialog box and put the settings in effect, click OK.

ADDING SCHEDULE ITEMS IN WEEKLY VIEW

You insert, move, delete, and edit appointments and events in Weekly view just as you do in Daily view. The only difference is how you view the items on the daily schedule. You have a better picture of how busy your schedule is for any given week when you switch over to Weekly view.

MAKING APPOINTMENTS ON THE WEEKLY TAB

You use the same methods for adding appointments to the Weekly view tab as you do in Daily view. You can insert appointments with the Insert New Appointment button on the toolbar, or you can add them directly to your schedule.

To add an appointment in Weekly view, follow these steps:

1. Double-click on the time slot where you want to add an appointment. This opens the Appointment dialog box. (You can also click on the Insert New Appointment button, or open the Insert menu and select Appointment.)

2. In the Appointment dialog box, set any start and ending times, type a description of the appointment, and include any options.

3. Click OK to exit the dialog box.

You can edit appointments at any time from Weekly view. Use the same editing techniques that you apply to appointments when you edit in Daily view.

- Double-click on the appointment to open the Appointment dialog box. You use this dialog box to make changes to the appointment.

- Another way to open the Appointment dialog box is to select the appointment and click on the Edit button on the toolbar.

- You can also make changes directly to the appointment as it appears on the schedule. Just click on the appointment you want to edit and make your changes to the text.

- Use the toolbar buttons to add reminders or to make your appointments private or tentative.

- You can use the editing commands and schedule options available on the Edit menu.

ADDING EVENTS IN WEEKLY VIEW

In Weekly view, each day has an Event icon at the top. You can use this icon just like the Event icon in Lesson 8. To insert an event to any day on your Weekly schedule, follow these steps:

1. Click on the Event icon at the top of the day to which you want to insert an event.

2. In the submenu that appears, choose the appropriate type of event. This opens an event dialog box.

3. In the Event or Annual Event dialog box, choose the event start date and end date, type in a description, and add any other options you want to apply.

4. Click OK to exit the dialog box.

You can edit and add new events to the Weekly view tab at any time. (Turn back to Lesson 8 for tips on scheduling events.)

VIEWING YOUR SCHEDULE BY MONTH

Want to see your entire month's worth of appointments? Switch over to Monthly view by clicking on the Monthly tab. Your screen opens, and you see the entire month, as shown in Figure 9.5.

Mind you, things are a little crowded in Monthly view. If you want to see details about any appointment listed in your schedule, double-click on the appointment. This opens the Appointment dialog box where you can see details about the appointment. If it's an event you want to see, double-click on it to open an event dialog box to view the details.

You can edit schedule items in Monthly view at any time; however, it's a little harder to see everything on-screen, so you're better off switching to Daily or Weekly view to do editing.

Left arrow button

Monthly tab

Use the scroll arrows to see other appointment times

Right arrow button

Appointments

FIGURE 9.5 Use the Monthly tab to view an entire month's worth of appointments.

CHANGING MONTHS

At the top of the Monthly view tab you see two arrow buttons (one on the left and one on the right), shown in Figure 9.5. Like the arrow buttons in Daily and Weekly view, you can use these to move your schedule view back or forward a month.

To change months, use any of these methods:

• To move forward to the next month, click once on the right arrow button.

• To move back to the previous month, click once on the left arrow button.

• If you hold down your mouse button while selecting the arrow buttons, you move quickly through the months of the year.

In this lesson, you learned how to view your schedule using the Weekly and Monthly tabs. In the next lesson, you'll learn how to use a To Do list.

LESSON 10

CREATING A TO DO LIST

In this lesson, you will learn how to create a To Do list to help you manage the tasks you need to keep track of on your daily schedule.

USING THE TO DO LIST

The To Do list is a handy feature that helps you organize the things you need to accomplish. You can use it to enter, manage, and track tasks and projects that are important to the various dates and appointments on your schedule. With the To Do list, you can assemble lists of daily things you need to do, items you must work on to complete a project, and even groceries you need to pick up on the way home. You can use the To Do list in all kinds of ways, but its main purpose is to help you keep track of things you need to do.

 Task Any item you list in the To Do list is a task. A task is something you need to take care of on a particular date, or something you need to do to complete a project.

Click on the To Do tab. This opens a To Do list on-screen, as shown in Figure 10.1.

You've already seen the To Do list in smaller scale on the Daily view tab. (Flip back to Daily view to see the To Do list in the bottom-right corner.) That particular list relates to the date you display on your Appointment Book schedule. It lists the tasks you need to complete that day, and any held-over tasks that you didn't complete the previous day. The To Do list in your To Do tab is the entire list of all the tasks you're tracking.

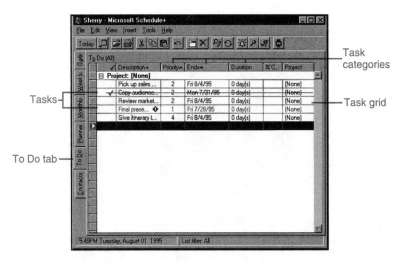

Tasks

To Do tab

Task categories

Task grid

FIGURE 10.1   The To Do tab.

WORKING WITH TASK CATEGORIES

As you can see in Figure 10.1, your big To Do list appears as a grid, and the more tasks you add, the bigger your grid gets. Schedule+ organizes the tasks into columns that represent categories (also called fields) such as task priority, end date, duration, and more. With these categories and others you might assign, you can organize the tasks into group and projects. You can even filter and sort your tasks.

CHANGING THE GRID DISPLAY

Schedule+ offers you several ways to control how it displays your To Do list grid. You can resize the columns to suit your needs. To change a column width, click on its border and drag it to a new location.

You can also change how the gridlines appear with the Options dialog box. Use these steps to turn the gridlines on or off:

1. Open the Tools menu and choose Options. This opens the Options dialog box, shown in Figure 10.2.

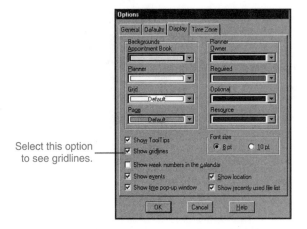

Select this option
to see gridlines.

Figure 10.2   The Options dialog box.

2. Click on the Display tab to bring this tab to the front of the dialog box.

3. Deselect the Show gridlines check box. (You remove the check mark from the box by selecting it.)

4. Click OK to exit the dialog box. The gridlines no longer show up in your To Do list.

5. To turn the gridlines on again, follow the same steps, but select the Show gridlines check box in step 3.

Changing Categories with the Columns Dialog Box

By default, Schedule+ shows several categories, or fields, that relate to the tasks you want to list. However, you can change the categories at any time. In the Columns dialog box, you can add and remove the task categories that appear on your grid.

If you don't like the task categories shown on the default grid, follow these steps to change the categories:

1. Open the View menu, select Columns, and select Custom.
   The Columns dialog box appears, as shown in Figure
   10.3.

2. You can change the categories Schedule+ displays. The
   Available fields list shows the remaining categories you
   can use. The Show these columns list shows what categories Schedule+ currently displays in your grid.

Here's a list of other task categories you can use.

This shows the columns Schedule+ currently displays in your grid.

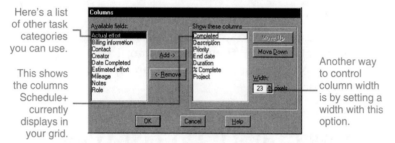

Another way to control column width is by setting a width with this option.

FIGURE 10.3   The Columns dialog box is where you can change
the task categories Schedule+ displays.

3. To add a category to the Show these columns list, click on
   the category on the left and click on the Add button. To
   remove a category from the Show these columns list,
   select the category and click on the Remove button.

4. To change the order of the categories, select the category
   to move and click on the Move Up or Move Down buttons until the category is in the desired location.

5. To exit the dialog box and go back to your To Do list grid,
   click on the OK button. Schedule+ reflects any changes
   you made in the Columns dialog box on your To Do list
   grid.

CHANGING CATEGORIES WITH THE COLUMNS COMMAND

For a faster change of your To Do list task categories, use the Columns submenu. Open the View menu and select Columns. In the

submenu that appears you have several category options available:

- If you want to show all the possible task categories in your grid, select All from the submenu that appears.

- To show a limited number of task categories, choose Few from the submenu.

- To go back to the original task categories in the display, choose Typical from the submenu.

- If you don't want to see any additional categories at all, click on Description from the submenu. This option leaves you with just the Completed and Description task categories.

READING THE TO DO LIST GRID

Take a look at Figure 10.4 to see what kinds of things the task grid tells you.

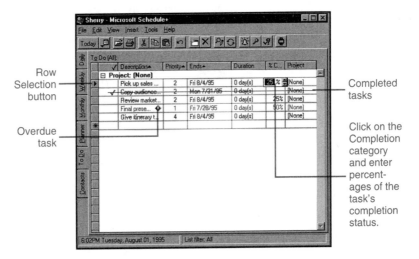

Row Selection button

Overdue task

Completed tasks

Click on the Completion category and enter percentages of the task's completion status.

FIGURE 10.4   You can indicate on your task list how close you are to completing each task.

- Completed tasks appear with a line through them and a check mark in the Completed column.

- Any tasks you have not completed by the specified end date appear with an overdue symbol next to them. Also, the dates for these tasks are marked in red so you can't miss them.

- If you're viewing the To Do list in the Daily view tab, note that uncompleted tasks from the previous day or days are held over and appear in red in the next day's To Do list.

- If you sort your tasks (which you'll learn to do in Lesson 11), you see an arrow next to the heading; it shows the direction in which you sorted the tasks. An up arrow means you sorted the tasks in ascending order, and a down arrow means you sorted the tasks in a descending order.

- You can group your tasks under project headings (see Lesson 11). The symbols (plus or minus signs) in front of the project heading enable you to hide or display the tasks related to the project. The project shown in Figure 10.4 has a minus sign next to its project heading, which means Schedule+ is displaying all the tasks.

- Some categories, when selected, open boxes for changing dates or percentages. These come in handy when you edit the progress and status information about your task.

- Use the Row Selection button to select an entire row.

Cells, Fields, and Records Tables such as the one shown in the Schedule+ To Do list consist of intersecting columns and rows that form *cells*. Each row and column represents a *heading/entry* or *field/record*. In databases, which is what the To Do list is, each column is a field and each row is a record.

ADDING TASKS

It's time to start adding your own tasks to the list. A task can be any item you want to accomplish or track. To add a task to your own To Do list, follow these steps:

1. Click on the To Do tab to bring it to the front. Choose a row in which to start entering your task.

2. Click on the Description column and type in a description for your task.

3. Continue adding information in each category for the task until you fill in everything that's relevant, such as a due date for completing the task or a time range for how long you can work the task. (You can press the Tab key to advance to each category in the row, or you can click on the cells using your mouse.)

USING THE TASK DIALOG BOX

A second way to add tasks to your To Do list is with the Task dialog box. This dialog box enables you to add more detailed information about your task to the To Do list. Use these steps to add a task with the Task dialog box:

1. There are two ways to open the Task dialog box: you can double-click on the Row Selection button in front of the task (see Figure 10.4), or you can click on the Insert New Task button on your toolbar. Either method opens the Task dialog box, shown in Figure 10.5.

Task Shortcut Another way to open the Task dialog box
- TIP - is to right-click on the grid and select New Task.

2. In the General tab, enter an ending date in the Active range area associated with the task, or select a date with the arrows in the drop-down list. You can also specify a starting date, which helps you track the duration of the task.

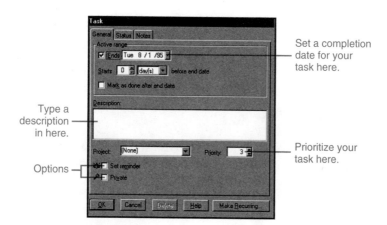

Set a completion date for your task here.

Type a description in here.

Options

Prioritize your task here.

FIGURE 10.5   The Task dialog box. It is very similar to the Appointment dialog box.

3. Use the Mark as done after end date check box to auto-matically mark the task when you complete it. By the way, this feature marks the tasks as completed after a period of time regardless of whether you remember to or not.

4. Type a description of your task in the Description text box.

5. If you want to associate the task with a specific project, type the project's name in the Project text box. (You learn more about projects in Lesson 11.)

6. If you want to prioritize the task, mark a priority rating in the Priority text box. By default, Schedule+ assigns a number 3, or normal, priority rating, but you can change this to another rating at any time.

7. If you need a reminder to alert you about a task, set one with the Set Reminder check box and specify when you want the reminder to appear.

8. If you don't want anyone else viewing your task, click on the Private option.

9. Click OK to exit the dialog box and return to the To Do
   list; your new task appears on the grid.

You can use the Status tab and the Notes tab in the Task dialog
box to add additional information about your task. You can also
click on the Make Recurring button to turn a task into a recurring
item.

In this lesson, you learned how to use and insert tasks in the To
Do list. In the next lesson, you'll learn how to group tasks into
projects and track the progress of projects.

WORKING WITH TASKS AND PROJECTS

In this lesson, you will learn how to group tasks into projects and keep track of the projects in your schedule.

TURNING TASKS INTO PROJECTS

With Schedule+, you can group your tasks under a particular project name to help you organize the things you need to do. Let's say your boss put you in charge of creating a company brochure highlighting products and services. To accomplish a project like this, you have to complete many individual tasks, such as writing the copy to include inside the brochure, designing the layout, creating artwork, proofreading the material, and arranging to have the brochure printed by a professional printer.

Schedule+ can help you keep track of these various tasks with the To Do list. By organizing the tasks under one project name as shown in Figure 11.1, you make it easier to locate, track, and see the tasks as you work on the project.

To create a project, follow this procedure:

1. Click the To Do tab to bring it to the front. Open the Insert menu and select Project, or right-click to open the shortcut menu and select New Project.

2. The Project dialog box opens (see Figure 11.2). Type a name for your project in the Name text box.

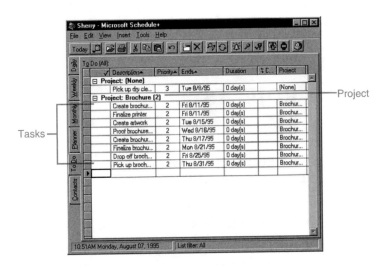

Tasks ─

Project

FIGURE 11.1   Schedule+ makes it easy to keep track of related tasks by listing them under project headings.

FIGURE 11.2   The Project dialog box.

3. You can prioritize your project with the Priority text box. Simply type in a priority assignment, or use the up and down arrows to set a different number.

4. If you want, you can turn the project into a private project using the Private check box. Click on the Private check box (a check mark indicates the feature is on) to hide the project.

5. Click OK to exit the dialog box. The project heading appears in the To Do list.

Once you have a project heading in place, you're ready to start adding tasks to it. To add tasks under the project heading, follow these steps:

1. To add new tasks to the project heading, open the Insert menu and select Task.

2. In the Task dialog box, type information pertaining to the task, such as an end date and a description.

3. To place the task under a project, click on the Project drop-down list, shown in Figure 11.3. Choose a project heading from the list.

The Project drop-down list shows current project headings in your schedule.

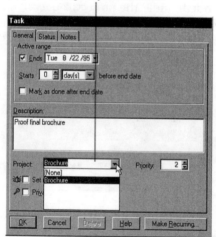

FIGURE 11.3   Use the Task dialog box to assign new tasks to your project heading.

4. To exit the dialog box and add the task under the project heading, click OK.

If you have tasks in your To Do list, you can easily list them under project headings, too. There are a couple of ways to do this:

- Select the task by clicking on the Row Selection button (at the left of each task) and drag it under the appropriate project heading.

- Open the Task dialog box (by double-clicking on the task) and assign a project heading to the task from the Project drop-down list.

DISPLAYING PROJECTS AND RELATED TASKS

When you have several projects on your To Do list, you can choose to list all the tasks under them, or hide the tasks. The tiny boxes in front of the project heading enable you to turn your project task list on or off. A minus sign means all your tasks are visible (or expanded) under the project; a plus sign means the tasks are hidden (or collapsed) in the list. Take a look at Figure 11.4 to see what the boxes look like.

Click here to hide or display tasks under a project heading.

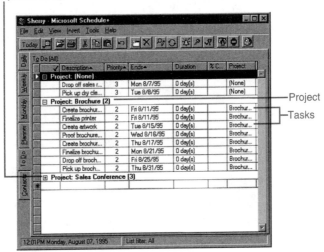

FIGURE 11.4 You can control how Schedule+ displays tasks under the project headings.

To hide the tasks under a project heading, click on the project heading box. This changes the minus sign to a plus sign. To display the tasks, click on the tiny box again.

GROUPING TASKS

Not only can you control how projects and tasks appear on the To Do list (hidden or displayed), but also you can control how Schedule+ groups and lists the projects and tasks. For example, you can choose to list tasks by completion dates or by priority. You can determine the order in which Schedule+ lists your tasks under a project heading. You can list tasks in ascending or descending order, and you can list the tasks based on information in your To Do list's categories.

The Group by dialog box enables you to group tasks in up to three levels or criteria. To group your tasks, follow these steps:

1. Double-click on the project heading, or open the View menu and select Group by. The Group by dialog box appears, as shown in Figure 11.5.

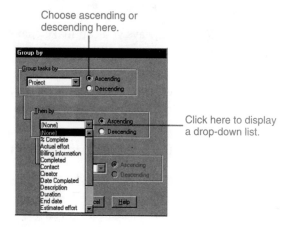

Choose ascending or descending here.

Click here to display a drop-down list.

FIGURE 11.5   The Group by dialog box.

2. Select the first Group tasks by drop-down list. Choose a category by which you want to group the tasks in your list. For example, if you want to view your list by the end dates that you finish each task, select End date as the category you want to group by.

3. Next, select how you want to display the categories, either in ascending or descending order. Click on the appropriate option button to make this selection.

4. You can group your tasks by yet another level of information. To do this, select a second category in the Then by drop-down list and follow the same procedure as in step 2. Continue selecting the categories for grouping the tasks in your list.

5. When you finish selecting the category or categories by which to group your tasks, click OK to exit the dialog box. Schedule+ rearranges the tasks according to your selections.

EDITING TASKS

There are all kinds of ways you can make changes to the tasks in your To Do list. Here are some methods you can use to edit tasks:

- You can double-click on the Row Selection button next to the task you want to edit and make your changes in the Task dialog box.

- You can select a specific task field and make your changes directly into the individual parts of your task in the list.

Edit the Daily To Do List, Too! You can apply the editing techniques listed here to your To Do list on the Daily view tab. You don't have to open the To Do tab every time you need to make changes.

- Depending on the column, additional controls appear when you click on a field. You can use the controls to set different percentages, dates, and so on. These controls are helpful in tracking the status of the tasks.

- You can right-click on your selected task to open a shortcut menu with more commands you can use to edit your task.

- To delete a task, select it and press the Delete key.

- Don't forget about those handy Cut, Copy, and Paste commands. You can select them from your toolbar or the Edit menu. (See Lesson 7 for more information.)

- To change your column headings (fields) open the View menu and select Column; then select Custom. This opens the Columns dialog box where you can edit which columns appear in your list. (See Lesson 10.)

- To display more or fewer columns, open the View menu, select Column, and select the number of columns you want to display on your grid.

- To insert a new row onto your grid, select the row before which you want the new row to appear, open the Insert menu, and choose Row.

TIP   **Turning Tasks into Appointments**   You can quickly turn a task into an appointment on your schedule. Select the task, right-click to display the shortcut menu, and select Appt. from Task. This opens the Appointment dialog box that you use to turn the task into an appointment.

SETTING TASK REMINDERS

You learned about setting reminders in your schedule in Lesson 6. You can also assign reminders to your tasks. If you add a reminder option to a task, you see a Daily Reminder box on your screen the day you need to work on a task. Task reminders work like the reminder message boxes you use with your daily appointments. However, task reminders appear at the beginning of the day, not at a specific time; Schedule+ associates task reminders with dates, not times.

For example, if you assign a specific date to a task and set up a task reminder option for that date, you can expect to see a task reminder box on that date as soon as you start your Schedule+ program.

To add a reminder to any task, follow these steps:

1. Double-click on the task for which you want to set a reminder from the To Do list. This opens the Task dialog box (refer to Figure 11.3).

2. Click on the Set Reminder check box (the one with the bell icon) and set how many days before or after the task date that you want to receive a reminder about the task. For example, if you want to receive a reminder about a task three days before its end date, set your reminder for three days and select **End date** from the drop-down list.

3. Click OK to exit the dialog box. A reminder icon now appears beside the task description in the To Do list.

On the day you set for the reminder to alert you of the task, the task reminder message box appears with an audible beep when you first start your Schedule+ program for the day. To close the message box, click OK. You can also choose to make changes, such as resetting the days, to the task reminder message box by clicking on the Edit button.

TRACKING TASKS

Tracking tasks on your To Do list is fairly straightforward. When you complete a task, click on the Completed column (the column with a check mark at the top). Schedule+ places a check mark in front of your task and strikes through the task with a line, and the % Complete column shows 100% (if you use a % Complete category). Take a look at Figure 11.6 to see what a completed task looks like.

Use this column to track how much
of the task you have completed.

Completed
column

Completed
task

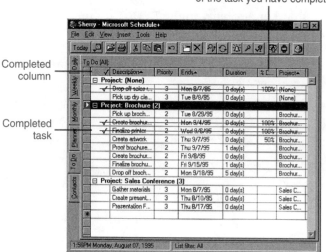

FIGURE 11.6 Use the To Do list's tracking features to help you monitor a task's status.

There are lots of ways for you to use the To Do list's task categories to track a task's status. Here are a few things to remember when tracking your tasks:

- If a project or task is related to a specific date on your schedule, it shows up in the Daily view tab on the To Do list.

- Any tasks that are left over from the day before appear in red with an overdue symbol next to them on the To Do list.

- The % Complete column enables you to log in a percentage that indicates how much of the task is complete.

- The Priority column enables you to prioritize the tasks based on a number scale.

- The Ends column specifies when you are to complete the task.

There's a great deal of flexibility in the To Do list's tracking features that enables to you maintain a system that works best for you. Although Schedule+ helps you by providing reminders and overdue icons, it's still up to you to manage your To Do list and keep yourself on schedule.

In this lesson, you learned how to list tasks under project headings, to group the tasks in the To Do list, and to track tasks. In the next lesson, you'll learn how to build a database of contacts.

BUILDING A CONTACTS LIST

In this lesson, you will learn how to use Schedule+ to build a list of the people you contact the most.

USING THE CONTACTS LIST

You use the contacts tab to compile information about the people, such as business associates, sales leads, friends, and neighbors, you contact the most. Once you complete your Contacts list, you can keep updating it and even use it to make appointments. You can also list birthdays or other special events associated with the contact so that the events appear on your schedule. If you use Schedule+ on a network, you can share your Contacts list with other users. Regardless of how you use it, you quickly find that the Contacts feature is an important part of your Schedule+ program.

The Contacts list that you build in Schedule+ is actually a database. A *database* is a collection of information that you can store, organize, and retrieve quickly. The information you store for each person is a *record*. The individual parts of the record, such as the name or address, are *fields*.

Database   A database is a computer program or feature designed to store, organize, and retrieve large collections of data.

You can use the names, addresses, and phone numbers from your Contacts list to create mailing lists, call up other computers (with a modem), and more. It's like having an electronic Rolodex at your fingertips.

To display the Contacts list, click on the Contacts tab on your Schedule+ window. This opens your program up to a screen similar to the one shown in Figure 12.1.

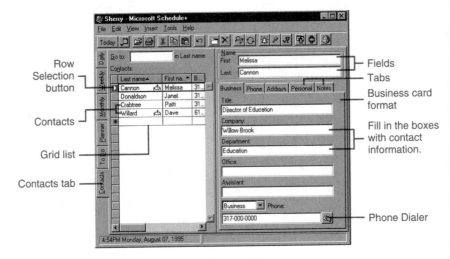

FIGURE 12.1   The Contacts tab.

As you look around the Contacts tab, you see a grid with a list of contacts on the left and a business card type area for entering data on the right. After you start a list of contacts, you can sort and group the contacts.

Here's what each of the Contacts tab features can do:

- Use the Go to text box to quickly locate contacts in your database. Type in the name of the person you're looking for, and Schedule+ highlights this person in your list.

- The Contacts area of the tab displays a grid list of your database names and fields.

- The Name area (in the business card area) displays a form in which you can enter information about your contact, such as the contact's name, business, phone number, and address.

You'll learn more about using each of these features later in this lesson.

ENTERING CONTACTS

You might as well jump right in and start compiling your own list of contacts. Remember, a contact can be anybody you know or with whom you do business. Contacts can include friends, relatives, coworkers, business associates, vendors, and more. You can enter information about your contacts directly into the grid list, or you can use the business card area of tabs and fields. Here's one way you can enter a contact into the list:

1. Click on a Row Selection button in front of the row you want to enter your contact into, preferably an empty row. This displays a blank Name form on the right side of your screen.

2. In the Name area, start typing information into each field as necessary. For example, to enter a name, click inside the First text box and type a first name.

3. If necessary, click on the Business tab to bring it to the front. Start filling in the Business tab fields. Click inside each text box, or field, to fill in related information. Keep in mind that you do not need to fill in every field, only the ones you use the most.

4. Click on the other business card tabs to enter more details, such as other phone numbers and addresses.

5. To enter birthday or anniversary information about the contact, click on the Personal tab, shown in Figure 12.2, and set the date. When you enter personal information about a contact (such as a birthday), a birthday cake symbol appears in your contact grid.

Personal tab

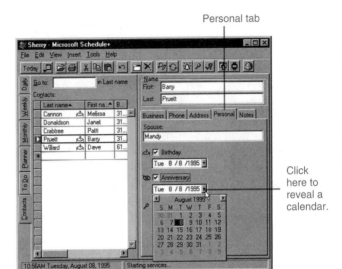

Click
here to
reveal a
calendar.

FIGURE 12.2   The Personal tab.

6. When you finish with the contact information, click inside the grid area. Your entry now appears as a contact on
the list, as shown in Figure 12.3.

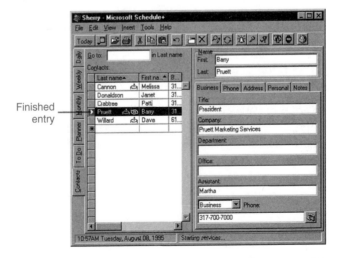

Finished
entry

FIGURE 12.3   A finished entry appears in the Contacts grid.

You can repeat these steps to continue adding new contacts to
your database.

ENTERING CONTACTS WITH THE CONTACT DIALOG BOX

If you don't like the direct approach to building a Contacts list,
you can use the Contact dialog box. This dialog box neatly displays similar fields from the form on the Contacts tab, but it
places the information in a larger area. To open the Contact dialog box, choose one of these methods:

- Open the Insert menu and select Contact.

- Right-click to display the shortcut menu and select New
  Contact.

- Double-click on an empty row's Row Selection button.

- Click on the Insert New Contact button on your toolbar.

All of these methods open the Contact dialog box, shown in
Figure 12.4.

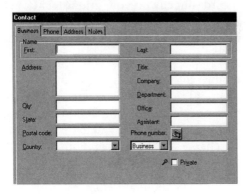

FIGURE 12.4 The Contact dialog box.

The dialog box looks like the business card area on your Contacts tab, only the information is spread out and arranged differently. However, you can't enter personal information about the contact in the Contact dialog box. You can only do this in the Personal tab on the Contacts tab of the program. The Contact dialog box does not include fields for birthdays or anniversaries.

To use the Contact dialog box, fill in each field in the tabs for which you have information. If you want to keep certain listings in your Contacts tab private, click on the Private check box in the Contact dialog box. This keeps the information hidden from other users on your Schedule+ network. Click OK when you finish to return to the Contacts tab.

EDITING CONTACTS

You can edit the records in your Contacts list at any time. You can make your changes directly into the grid list, in the business card area on the right, or with the Contact dialog box. You can also use the toolbar buttons and menus. Try any of these techniques to make changes to your own Contacts list:

- To edit records directly on your grid list, click inside the cell where you want to make changes. You use the scroll bars to move back and forth between the fields and records.

- To edit contact information directly in the business card area on the right side of the Contacts tab, select the record you want to change. This action displays the record's fields. Click inside any field on the right and make your changes to the information.

- Double-click on a row's Row Selection button to open the Contact dialog box and make changes.

- You can also display the Contact dialog box by right-clicking on the entry and choosing Edit Item from the shortcut menu, or by clicking on the Edit button on your toolbar.

As you work with your Contacts list over time, you may need to remove old contacts that you no longer need. To delete a contact, use any of these methods:

- Select the record by clicking on the record's Row Selection button (this highlights the entire record) and click on the Delete button on the toolbar.

- Double-click on the record's Row Selection button to open the Contact dialog box and click on the Delete button.

- Select the record using the Row Selection button, and press the Delete key on your keyboard.

- Select the record using the Row Selection button, open the Edit menu, and choose Delete Item.

- Right-click on the record to display a shortcut menu and select Delete Item.

In this lesson, you learned how to build and edit a Contacts list. In the next lesson, you'll learn how to sort and group your contacts.

13

LESSON

SORTING AND GROUPING CONTACTS

In this lesson, you will learn how to group and sort information in your Contacts list, and how to insert your contacts into appointments and tasks.

SORT THROUGH YOUR CONTACTS LIST

After you compile a list of contacts, you will want to be able to sort through the list, especially if it's a long list. When you perform a sort, Schedule+ looks through the database for specific records, fields, and common elements. You can then display those records that Schedule+ finds in a particular order.

There are several ways to sort your contacts. Let's start out with a simple sort in your Contacts grid. You can click on any of the column headings in your grid list to perform an immediate sort of data in that column, or field, in ascending order. For example, if you click on the First name column heading, Schedule+ immediately sorts the database alphabetically by first names and displays the records in ascending order (As at the top of the list and Zs at the bottom) as shown in Figure 13.1.

The up arrow on the column heading means that you sorted the selected column in ascending order. To sort in descending order (Z to A), press the Ctrl key while you click on the column heading. When you do this, Schedule+ sorts your list in descending order. Schedule+ determines the column headings that appear in your grid by the Group by settings, which you'll learn about later in this lesson.

The up arrow means Schedule+
sorted the list in ascending order.

Column
heading

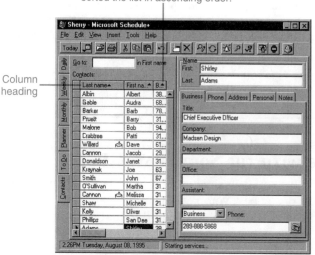

FIGURE 13.1   You can sort a Contacts list by last names.

That was an easy way to sort your information. There are a couple
of other ways you can sort. If you want to sort new entries immediately after you enter them, use the AutoSort command. Open
the View menu and select AutoSort. Anytime you type a contact,
Schedule+ automatically sorts it as soon as you finish entering it.
Yet another way you can sort data is with the Sort dialog box,
which you'll learn about next.

Go To   Don't forget about the Go to box at the top of
your Contacts tab. It's a speedy route to the fields Sched-
ule+ displays on your grid. (Remember, Schedule+
displays the columns you specify with the View, Group by
command. You'll learn about the Group by command later
in this lesson.)

Ascending or Descending? When you sort, there has to be some type of order to the list that Schedule+ displays in your grid: alphabetical or numerical. If you sort in ascending order, Schedule+ displays your records from A to Z or from 1 to the greatest numerical value in your list. If you sort in descending order, Schedule+ reverses the order alphabetically or numerically.

Sorting with the Sort Dialog Box

Now try another sort, this time using more details. When you sort with the Sort dialog box, you have the option of sorting by three levels and by several categories. In addition to these options, you can choose to view the sort in ascending or descending order. In each level, you can click on the drop-down arrow to reveal the category by which you wish to conduct the sort.

All of the categories Schedule+ displays in the drop-down list are actually fields from your Contacts tab. The Sort feature enables you to choose to sort by any field available on the Contacts tab or the Contact dialog box.

You can use the Sort dialog box to be very specific about how Schedule+ displays your contacts in the grid list. For example, perhaps you want to sort your Contacts list by ZIP code (called *postal code* in Schedule+). In the Sort box drop-down lists, you have the choice of sorting by business address postal codes or home address postal codes. Schedule+ has a great deal of flexibility in its sorting capabilities.

To sort your contacts using the Sort dialog box, follow these steps:

1. Open the View menu and select Sort.

2. This opens the Sort dialog box you use to determine how you want to arrange the list. You can sort your Contacts list using up to three different levels, shown in Figure 13.2. Select the first sort level.

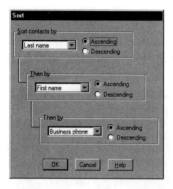

FIGURE 13.2   Start with the first sort level and select a category to sort your list by.

3. Click on the drop-down arrow in the Sort Contacts by drop-down list to display sort categories, and then choose a category from the list.

4. Continue choosing levels and categories from the Then by drop-down lists to narrow your sort.

5. Click OK to exit the dialog box and perform the sort on your list.

Also on the View menu is a Sort Now command that immediately sorts your list based on specifications you set in the Sort dialog box.

GROUPING CONTACTS

Do many of your contacts share the same information, such as phone numbers or departments? Another thing you can do with your list is group your contacts. For instance, because some of the people on your list work for the same company or same industry, you can group them together. The Schedule+ grouping feature enables you to group contacts in a variety of categories and sub-groups.

To group contacts, follow these steps:

1. Open the View menu and select Group By. This opens the Group by dialog box, shown in Figure 13.3.

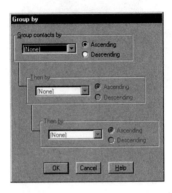

FIGURE 13.3   The Group by dialog box.

2. Open the Group Contacts by drop-down list by clicking the arrow, and select a category with which you want to group your contacts. Schedule+ bases these categories on fields in your Contacts tab. The categories that you choose to group by in your list also determine which columns Schedule+ displays on the grid.

3. Choose additional categories to group by from the Then by drop-down lists.

4. Choose ascending or descending order for each category you select.

5. Click OK to exit the dialog box and display your groups. The grid list now displays the groups that you specified, as shown in Figure 13.4. The group name appears in bold above each group of contacts on the list.

All of these contacts use the
same business address.

Group
name

Group
symbols

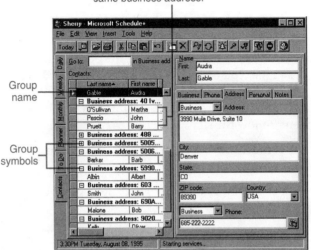

FIGURE 13.4 In this example, I grouped my contacts list by
business addresses.

6. You can expand or collapse the list in a group by clicking
   on the group symbol (the tiny box) in front of the group
   name. A minus sign in the tiny box in front of the group
   name means that every contact is visible. A plus sign in
   the tiny box means that every contact pertaining to the
   group name is hidden. Click on the plus or minus sign to
   show or hide contacts listed under the group name.

7. To ungroup your Contacts list, open the Group by dialog
   box again, this time selecting None for each Group by
   category.

USING CONTACT INFORMATION IN APPOINTMENTS OR TASKS

After compiling a list of contacts, you can use the Contacts list to schedule appointments or tasks to use with the other Schedule+ features. For example, you can select a contact from your list and use the information about the contact to create an appointment on your daily schedule. To use contact information to schedule an appointment, follow the steps below:

1. Select the contact with whom you want schedule an appointment.

2. Right-click to open the shortcut menu and choose Appt. from Contact.

3. The Appointment dialog box appears on-screen, as shown in Figure 13.5. The Description box shows your contact's name and company. Set a time and date for the appointment.

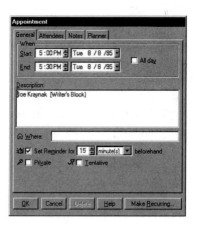

FIGURE 13.5   The Appointment dialog box.

4. Click OK to exit the dialog box, and Schedule+ inserts the appointment in your schedule.

To use contact information in a task, follow these steps:

1. Select the contact about whom you need information for a task on your To Do list.

2. Right-click to open the shortcut menu and choose Task from Contact.

3. The Task dialog box appears on-screen, and its Description box shows your contact's name and company. Add any options you want to include in the task, such as an end date or reminder.

4. If the task is related to a specific project, identify that project heading with the Project drop-down list.

5. Click OK to exit the dialog box, and Schedule+ adds the contact information to the task on your To Do list.

DIAL 'EM UP!

You may notice a tiny phone icon in the Contacts tab or in the Contact dialog box. This is the Dial Phone button, and it's part of the Phone Dialer feature, a Windows 95 accessory program. The Dial Phone button enables you to use your computer modem to call your contact's modem or fax machine. You can use the little phone symbols that appear next to phone numbers to dial up your contacts. Just click on the Dial Phone button, and your computer starts dialing for you, as shown in Figure 13.6.

FIGURE 13.6   The Dial Phone button automatically starts dialing with your modem.

Your phone must be hooked up to a modem for this to work. You also need to make sure your modem is set up properly. (You can set up the modem settings in the Windows 95 Control Panel. Just click on the Modems icon to open up the options.) To open the Windows 95 Phone Dialer feature, open the Accessories menu and select Phone Dialer. You can also dial your contacts directly with the Phone Dialer window.

 Warning! The Dial Phone button does not enable you to place ordinary phone calls. You can only make calls using your computer's modem.

In this lesson, you learned how to work with your Contacts list, grouping and sorting the list and using the Phone Dialer feature. In the next lesson, you'll learn how to print portions of your schedule.

PRINTING YOUR SCHEDULE

*In this lesson, you will learn how to preview and
print portions of your schedule, including appointments, To Do lists,
and the Contacts list.*

PRINTING WITH SCHEDULE+

Being able to print out portions of your schedule is an important
part of using Schedule+. There are times when you aren't sitting
in front of your computer with your daily schedule ready to use.
You may have to travel or work at home, and you want a copy of
your schedule on hand. Or perhaps you need to give a friend or
co-worker a copy of your To Do list or Contacts list.

Schedule+ offers you several ways to print portions of the various
features. You find all the options listed in the Print dialog box,
shown in Figure 14.1.

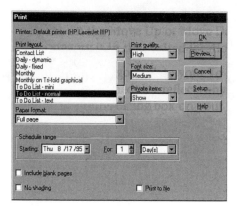

FIGURE 14.1   The Print dialog box.

ELEMENTS OF THE PRINT DIALOG BOX

Let's go over the Print dialog box in more detail so you can learn how to use its options. Take a look at the Print dialog box again in Figure 14.2. This time callouts label the elements of the dialog box to show you what each element controls.

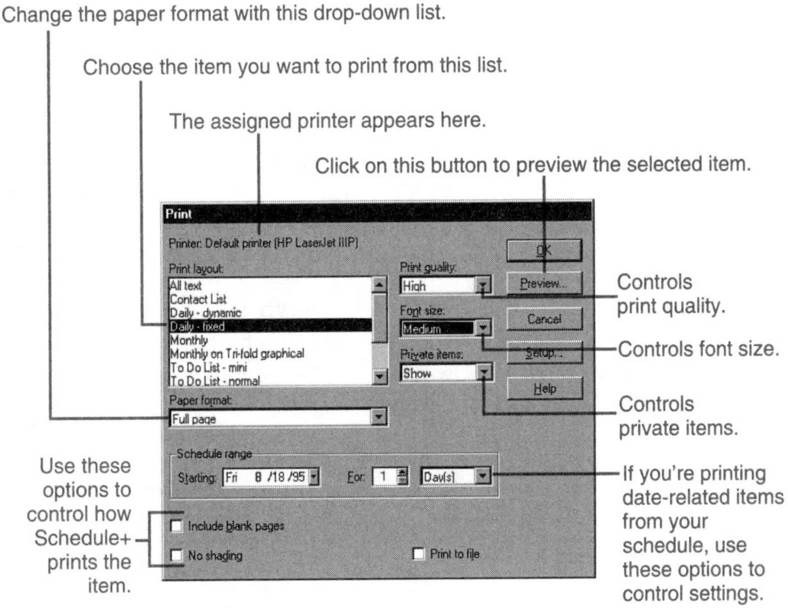

Change the paper format with this drop-down list.

Choose the item you want to print from this list.

The assigned printer appears here.

Click on this button to preview the selected item.

FIGURE 14.2   Each part of the Print dialog box controls how Schedule+ prints your item.

- At the top of the dialog box, you find a listing for your default printer. To change this to another printer, click on the Setup button and select another printer from the Printer drop-down list box.

- The Print layout list box lists all the parts of your Schedule+ program that you can print out. Use the scroll bar to view different items in the list. (More about this later in the lesson.)

- The Paper format drop-down list box enables you to choose to print the selected item on paper, a Filofax page (a personal organizer), or on labels.

- The Schedule range options enable you to select the date(s) you print out for the selected item (when applicable). For example, if you're printing your weekly schedule, you can choose the exact week you want to print out.

- The options at the bottom of the dialog box enable you to control how Schedule+ prints the item. For example, if you select the No shading check box, the top of your printout isn't shaded with the default design (which tends to use up a lot of your printer's ink).

- The three drop-down list boxes to the right of the Print layout list box enable you to control print quality, font size, and private items on your schedule.

- Use the Preview command button to preview how the selected item looks before printing it out. (Learn more about this feature later in this lesson.)

Speedy Printing By default, Schedule+ prints each item with shaded areas (sometimes these areas are located at the top of the page; other times they're scattered on your page). To speed up printing, be sure to select the No shading check box. This keeps the printer from printing the shaded background, which makes it easier for you to read the text from the shaded areas.

USING THE PRINT LAYOUT LIST BOX

The Print layout list box displays the parts of your Schedule+ program you can select for printing. Simply highlight the layout you want to print and click on the OK button to print it out. By default, the dialog box is set up to print a full page of the selected item in its current date.

Each of the items in the Print layout list box enables you to print certain portions of your Schedule+ features. To use these items effectively, you need to know what each item prints. Table 14.1 explains what kind of printout you receive after selecting the item for printing.

TABLE 14.1   PRINT LAYOUT LIST BOX OPTIONS

OPTION	RESULT
All text	Prints out all the text items in your daily schedule.
Contact List	Prints the entire list of contacts you have in the Contacts List.
Daily—dynamic	Prints the daily schedule in its most current state of change on your network.
Daily—fixed	Prints the daily schedule.
Monthly	Prints the monthly view of your schedule.
Monthly on Tri-fold graphical	Prints three elements on a single page, including the daily schedule, all 12 months, and the To Do list.
To Do List—mini	Prints the tasks associated with the selected date.
To Do List—normal	Prints the entire To Do list, including all the details associated with each task.
To Do List—text	Only prints the text descriptions of the tasks.

OPTION	RESULT
Weekly 5 day	Prints five days of the week on a single page.
Weekly 7 day	Prints seven days of the week on a single page.

There are a few additional details to keep in mind when printing the different layouts:

- All tentative appointments that you schedule appear in italics on the printout.

- If you scheduled lots of appointments in the daily schedule you print, the appointments may not fit in the designated space. If this happens, you find that Schedule+ carries the overflow of appointments into the Other Appointments box on the printout.

- If you print the To Do list or Contacts list, the printout reflects any sorts you performed on the columns.

PREVIEWING YOUR SCHEDULE

One of the best parts of the Print dialog box in Schedule+ is the Preview feature. It enables you to see what your information looks like in printed form before you actually go to the trouble of printing it out. The Print Preview window enables you to preview any of the layout items in the Print layout list box. Follow these steps to preview your layout:

1. Open the Print dialog box. (Click on the Print button on the toolbar, or open the File menu and select Print.)

2. In the Print layout list box, choose the item you want to print. Click on the layout to highlight the selection.

3. Choose any additional options you want to apply.

4. When you're ready to preview the layout, click on the Preview button.

5. The Print Preview window appears on-screen, as shown in Figure 14.3. Use the scroll bars to view different portions of the layout.

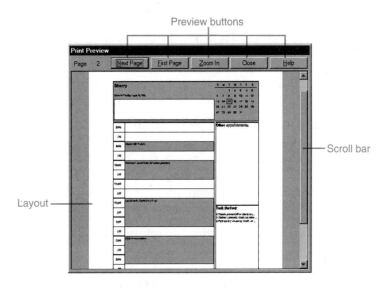

FIGURE **14.3**   The Print Preview window.

6. You can use the First Page and Next Page buttons at the top of the window to view other pages. Click on the Zoom In button to get a closer look, as shown in Figure 14.4.

7. To zoom back out again, click on the Zoom Out button.

8. When you're ready to exit the Print Preview window, click on the Close button to return to the Print dialog box.

The schedule name always appears at the top of the printout.

Any events you scheduled appear here.

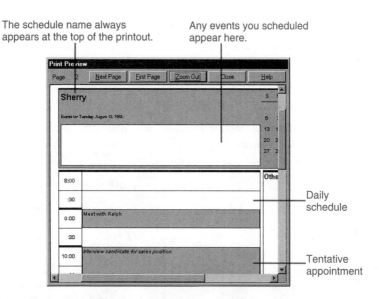

Daily schedule

Tentative appointment

FIGURE 14.4   You can get a better look at the layout's contents by using the zoom control.

Remember, the layout you see in the Print Preview window varies depending on the item you select in the Print layout list box. You can preview To Do lists, Contacts Lists, and more.

PRINTING YOUR SCHEDULE

Depending on what layout you select, your printout shows different elements and page orientation. You may be quite surprised by the professional-looking printout that comes out of your printer. In the top-left corner of every page is the schedule name (usually your name, if that's the schedule you chose to print). At the very bottom of the printed page, you find a footer (text line) indicating when you printed the page, complete with date and time.

To print out a copy of your schedule or any other Schedule+ features, follow these steps:

1. Open the Print dialog box by pulling down the File menu and selecting Print. (You can also access the box by clicking on the Print button on the toolbar.)

2. The Print dialog box appears on your screen. Select the layout you want to print from the Print layout list box. (Click on the item to highlight it.)

3. If necessary, select from any of the other printing options.

4. Click OK, and Schedule+ prints the schedule layout you selected.

What's the Print to File Option For? You can print other schedules besides the one you open in your program, such as another user's schedule on a network. Select the Print to File option; this opens a dialog box that enables you to choose other schedules to print. You can also use this option to save your own schedule in another folder or file.

In this lesson, you learned how to print parts of your schedule and other items. In the next lesson, you'll learn how to work with the Planner.

WORKING WITH THE PLANNER

In this lesson, you will learn how to use the Planner tab to view your schedule at a glance.

USING THE PLANNER TAB

For a different perspective of your busy schedule, take a look at it in Planner view. Click on the Planner tab on the left side of your view area. This opens your schedule in Planner view, as shown in Figure 15.1.

By default, the Planner view shows the schedule for several days as soon as you open it. However, you can change which days and weeks are in view, and you can change the size of each date's space on-screen.

The Planner enables you to see a graphical display of your schedule in chunks of time. This graphical depiction is called the *free/ busy display*. Like the Daily and Weekly views, the Planner view shows your schedule with a vertical display of time increments. Instead of sorting through individual appointments on the schedule, you can easily see your scheduled commitments spread out over several days. If you open the Planner view tab after using any of the other scheduling tabs, the Planner displays the same time and dates as the previous view tab.

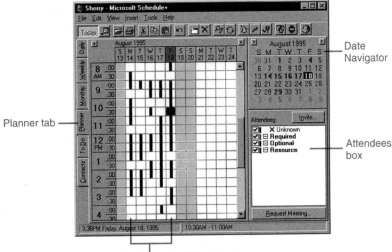

FIGURE 15.1 Planner view organizes your schedule into free and busy blocks of time.

Also on your screen is the Date Navigator, which you may recognize from the Daily view tab, and an Attendees box, which lists the other networked users that you invite to the meetings you schedule. You use the Attendees box only when you're networked with other Schedule+ users. (You learn more about using the Attendees box in Lesson 17.)

If you use the Planner view in group-enabled mode (on a network), you see a few different buttons on your screen. The Invite and Request Meeting buttons enable you to setup meetings with other network users. (You'll learn how to use these buttons in Lessons 16 and 17.) If you use the Planner tab in stand-alone mode (not on a network), you don't see an Invite button, and instead of the Request Meeting button, your screen shows a New Appointment button. You use the New Appointment button to schedule new appointments on your schedule. If you click on it, Schedule+ opens the Appointment dialog box, described in Lesson 5.

With the Planner view, you find that it's a lot easier to look at your schedule when it's spread out in blocks of time over several days. You can easily point out available time blocks. If you're networked, you can view other users' Planner views to help you organize meetings for all attendees.

 Hey, This Planner Looks Familiar   If you already peeked at the Planner tab in the Appointment dialog box, you've seen this feature already. Of course, it was a scaled-down view, but it was still the Planner.

CHANGING THE PLANNER DISPLAY

The Planner view shows the schedule for several days as soon as you open it. However, you can change which days and weeks are in view, and you can also change the size of three main elements on-screen.

To change the dates in view on the Planner tab, use any of these methods, which are pointed out on FIgure 15.2.

- Click on the left arrow button to move the view back one week.

- Click on the right arrow button to move the view forward one week.

- To return your view to the current date, click on the Today button on the toolbar.

- Use the Date Navigator to select a specific date to view. Just click on the day you want to see in the Date Navigator's calendar. To change the month the Date Navigator displays, click on the left or right arrow buttons in the corners of the calendar.

- You can also view a day quickly with the Go To Date button on the toolbar. This button works the same as the Date Navigator calendar.

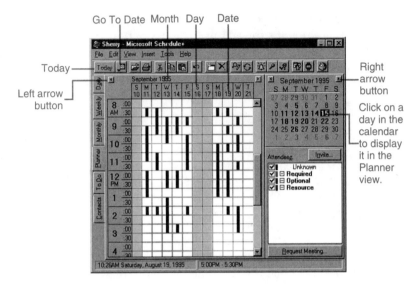

FIGURE 15.2   Schedule+ offers you many ways to change the dates that you see in the Planner view.

 TIP   **Shortcut Menu!**   To quickly view dates in the Planner view, right-click on the Date Navigator calendar. When the shortcut menu appears, select the Today or Go To command.

CHANGING THE SIZES OF PLANNER ELEMENTS

You can enlarge the amount of space each of the three elements of the Planner view takes up. For example, if you want to see more of the schedule and less of the Date Navigator and Attendees box, you can use your mouse to drag the border separating the elements to a new dimension. Follow these steps to resize any of the elements:

1. Move your mouse pointer over the border separating the elements you want to enlarge or reduce. The mouse

pointer turns into a double-headed arrow when you place it over a border, as shown in Figure 15.3.

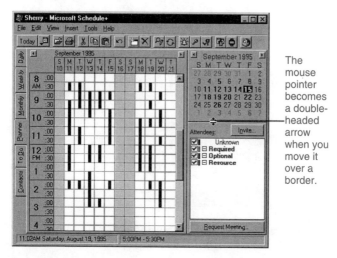

The mouse pointer becomes a double-headed arrow when you move it over a border.

Figure 15.3   Drag the borders to resize the elements in the Planner view.

2. Hold down the left mouse button and drag the pointer in the direction you want to enlarge or reduce.

3. Let go of the mouse button, and Schedule+ resizes the elements.

Reading the Planner Schedule

Before you can use the Planner feature effectively, you need to know how to read the blocks of time it displays on-screen. Depending on your setup (networked or not networked), the Planner reveals different items on-screen. While the Planner is very helpful in stand-alone mode, it is even more useful in a network situation. Planner view uses these helpful features:

• The blue lines, called bars, represent your appointments (see Figure 15.4). You can quickly see at a glance what times you are busy.

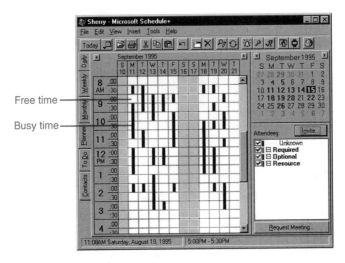

Free time

Busy time

FIGURE 15.4   The blue bars represent your busy times.

- The vertical gaps between the blue bars represent open chunks of time. This view enables you to see when you're available for other appointments or commitments.

- To see the details about a particular appointment, double-click on one of the bars. This reveals whose appointment it is. Click on the name to see details about the appointment.

- If you work in stand-alone mode (not connected to other computer users), your screen shows a New Appointment button. You can use the New Appointment button to quickly set another appointment on your schedule.

- If you work in group-enabled mode (networked with other users), your screen shows a Request Meeting button. You can use this button to invite other networked users to your meetings.

In this lesson, you learned how to use the Planner tab to view busy and free times on your schedule. In the next lesson, you'll learn how to use Schedule+ in a network environment.

Using Schedule+ on a Network

*In this lesson, you will learn how to use Schedule+
on a network and set up access permissions for others to view your
schedule.*

Working with Access Permissions

The Planner tab, described in Lesson 15, becomes extra useful
when you're networked with other Schedule+ users. It enables
you to see the busy schedules of others, coordinate meetings, and
track responses of attendees. In this lesson, you learn to set up
your schedule for viewing and accessing on a network.

Using Group-Enabled Mode The first time you open
Schedule+, you have the option of using the program in
group-enabled or stand-alone mode. If you're using
Schedule+ on a network, be sure to select group-enabled
mode. If you select the Don't ask me this question again
check box, you won't be able to switch to another mode
unless you reinstall Schedule+.

If you're using group-enabled mode, you can use the Planner view
to check out the scheduled blocks of time of other users who
publish their schedules on the network. You must have Read permission in order to see the schedules of other users, because after
all, they don't want just anybody knowing how busy—or not-so-
busy—they are. The same goes for you; you probably don't want
everyone on the network to have full access to your schedule. So
the first step in viewing schedules on a network is establishing
access permissions.

Viewing Access Permissions

Schedule+ enables you to use different levels of access permissions to view other users' schedules and let others view your schedule. The level of access permission depends upon what role you assign to the user. Table 16.1 shows the various roles and levels available.

Table 16.1 Access Permissions

Role	Permissions
None	No viewing permissions.
Read	Ability to read all appointments, contacts, tasks, events, and appointment details.
Create	Ability to set up appointments, add to contacts, tasks, and events.
Modify	Ability to make changes to appointments, contacts, tasks, and events.
Delegate	Ability to make changes to parts of schedule, except private items. Can also send and receive meeting messages on your behalf.
Owner	Ability to make changes to the schedule, view and change private items, and change users' permissions to access your schedule.
Delegate Owner	Same access as Owner; can also send and receive meeting messages for you.
Custom	You specify what permissions you want to allow.

Obviously, you can control how much of your schedule others on the network can access. All of these roles for other users depend on your own network or office situation. For example, if you're a busy executive, you may want to assign your secretary the role of Delegate Owner in order to keep your schedule organized. In this role, your secretary can make changes to your schedule, coordinate meetings, and control the access permissions that others have to your schedule. On the other hand, another executive in another department may only want to assign his secretary to the role of Read when it comes to accessing his schedule. Or, a team of co-workers may want to grant each other equal or varying roles regarding each individual's schedule.

To view users' access permissions, follow these steps:

1. Open the Tools menu and select Set Access Permissions.

2. This opens the Set Access Permissions dialog box, shown in Figure 16.1. To assign or view access permissions, click on the Users tab.

FIGURE 16.1   The Set Access Permissions dialog box.

3. To add other users to your list, click on the Add button. This opens the Add Users dialog box, shown in Figure 16.2.

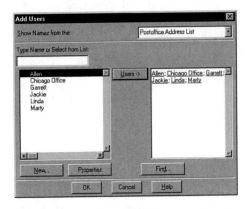

FIGURE 16.2 The Add Users dialog box enables you to add other network users' names to the Users list in the Set Access Permissions dialog box.

4. Choose the name you want to add from the list of users shown in the left column, or type the user's name. To select names from a specific network postoffice, select the address list from the Show Names drop-down list and choose the specific user name you want to add.

5. Click on the Users button to add the name to the right column list. The right column shows the names of users whose schedules you can currently view in the Planner tab.

6. Continue following steps 4 and 5 to add more names. Click OK to exit the Add Users box and add the name(s) to the Users list in the Set Access Permissions dialog box.

7. The Set Access Permissions dialog box reflects your changes. Click OK to exit the dialog box.

CHANGING ACCESS PERMISSIONS

You can change the access permissions that others have to your schedule at any time. Use these steps to change permissions:

1. Open the Tools menu and select Set Access Permissions.

2. This opens the Set Access Permissions dialog box (Figure 16.3). To assign or change access permissions, click on the Users tab.

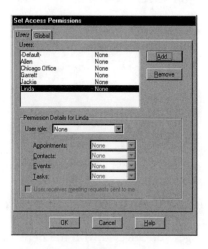

FIGURE 16.3 The Set Access Permissions dialog box lists users and their access permission status.

3. A list of users and their access permissions appears in the Users list box. Select the name of the person whose access you want to modify.

 The User Name Isn't Shown! If the user's name doesn't appear in the list box, click on the button and choose the user's name from your network mail list. Then click OK to return to the dialog box.

4. To assign a new predefined role, click on the User role drop-down list box, as shown in Figure 16.4. Select a role from the list.

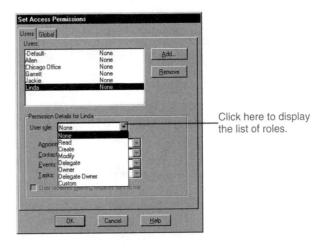

Click here to display the list of roles.

FIGURE 16.4   Select a new role from User role drop-down list.

5. Click on the OK button to exit the dialog box. (A warning box pops up on-screen telling you that Schedule+ is merging the changes you selected with the network's server.)

To customize the roles you assign, select the Custom role option in the User role drop-down list. Next you apply any of the following permission options, which appear below the User role drop-down list:

- Click on the Appointments list box to select the level of access you want the person to have to your appointments.

- Click on the Contacts list box to select the kind of access you want the person to have to your contacts.

- Click on the Events list box to choose the access permission you want the person to have to your events.

- Click on the Tasks list box to assign the permission role you want the person to have regarding your To Do list.

SCHEDULE POSTING OPTIONS

To control which parts of your schedule you post on the network, use the Global tab of the Set Access Permissions dialog box. Here you can choose to allow overlapping appointments or recurring appointments, and you can designate how much of your schedule you want to publish on the network. Follow these steps to change global access to your schedule:

1. Open the Tools menu and select Set Access Permissions.

2. This opens the Set Access Permissions dialog box. Click on the Global tab to bring this tab to the front of the dialog box, as shown in Figure 16.5.

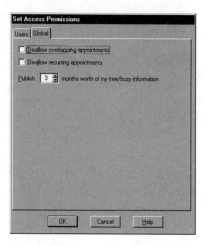

FIGURE 16.5   The Global tab of the Set Access Permissions dialog box has options for displaying your schedule on the network.

3. If you prefer not to allow overlapping appointments in your schedule, click on the Disallow overlapping appointments check box.

4. If you prefer not to let others set up recurring appointments in your schedule, click on the Disallow recurring appointments check box.

5. You can control how many months of your schedule you post on the network with the Publish option. Choose **0** if you do not want to post your schedule at all.

6. Click OK to exit the dialog box and put the options into effect.

Opening Other Users' Schedules

If you have access, you can open another user's schedule. Depending on what kind of permission you have, you might be able to do more than just read the schedule. In many instances, you may be in charge of managing the user's schedule or maintaining a task list or Contacts list. If you have the proper permissions, once you open the other person's schedule, you can make changes to it and add new items.

To open another schedule, besides your own, use these steps (these steps only apply to networked Schedule+ users):

1. Pull down the File menu and choose Open. In the submenu that appears, choose Other's Appointment Book.

2. The Open Other's Appt. Book dialog box appears, as shown in Figure 16.6. Select the name of the person whose schedule you want to open.

 I Don't See the Person's Name in the List! If the name of the person whose schedule you want to open doesn't appear in the list box, click on the Show Names drop-down list and choose the address list containing the name of the person you want. You can also use the Find button to look up the name.

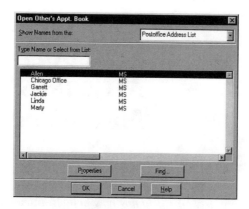

FIGURE 16.6   The Open Other's Appt. Book dialog box.

3. Click OK to exit the dialog box, and the schedule appears as a second opened program window in addition to your own schedule window. If it doesn't, you may not have the correct access role to open the other person's schedule.

Once you open another user's schedule, you can read or make changes to it only if you have the proper access. You don't see items marked as private unless the user assigned you Owner or Delegate Owner access.

To close the schedule at any time, use the same methods you use to close your own Schedule+ program:

• Click on the Close button in the upper-right corner.

• Open the File menu and select Exit.

• Double-click on the window's Control-menu icon (upper-left corner).

In this lesson, you learned how to view and change access permissions as well as open other users' schedules. In the next lesson, you'll learn how to schedule meetings in a network environment.

PREPARING TO SCHEDULE MEETINGS ON A NETWORK

In this lesson, you will learn the preparation steps you need to schedule a meeting on your network, including how to invite attendees and pick a time for the meeting.

SCHEDULING GROUP MEETINGS

When you use Schedule+ in a network environment, you can schedule meetings with other users on your network. It's easy and fast, and you can coordinate the best possible meeting times, track responses to your meeting invitations, and reschedule appointments with minimal effort.

To actually invite someone to a meeting, you send the person an e-mail message describing the event and requesting attendance. You can even e-mail meeting invitations to people outside of your network environment, as long as they use Microsoft Exchange to receive and send e-mail messages. (Although Schedule+ is useful for automating the scheduling and tracking of meetings with attendees outside your network, it is not required.) For example, if you're setting up a seminar, and you want to invite colleagues from other companies, Schedule+ can help you arrange the event and send out e-mail invitations.

When you schedule a meeting, there are several steps you have to go through before you can finalize the meeting on every participant's schedule. Look at this overview of the procedures you need to follow to schedule network meetings.

1. Initially, you need to determine who needs to attend the meeting. After you do this, you can view the schedules of the people you want to attend the meeting using the Invite button on the Planner tab. This button adds other users' schedules to your Planner view to enable you to see busy and free times.

2. Next, you need to check everybody's schedules for an available time in which you can all meet. When it comes to finding an appropriate meeting time, Schedule+ has several ways to help you. You can choose a meeting time by manually viewing schedules in the Planner view until you find a good time, or you can use the AutoPick feature to automatically coordinate an available time among all the attendees.

3. After you find a meeting time, you need to send out a Meeting Request. You use Schedule+'s Meeting Request form to send out request messages to everyone you want to attend the meeting. (More about this feature in Lesson 18.)

4. Finally, you can track everybody's responses to your request and find out who's attending the meeting and who's not (see Lesson 18).

One of the easiest ways to set up a meeting is to use Schedule+'s Meeting Wizard, a step-by-step approach to arranging a meeting from start to finish. (You learn more about this feature in Lesson 18.)

USING THE INVITE BUTTON

The first step to preparing a meeting with other users on your network is to determine who needs to attend the meeting. You can use the Invite button on the Planner tab to view other users' free and busy times in the Planner view. The Invite button does not invite people to the meeting, it just enables you to see everybody's schedule at a glance.

When creating an attendance list for a meeting, indicate which of the following categories each attendee falls into:

- **Required** These are the people whom you require to attend the meeting, and who are essential for the meeting's success. When the attendee notes that you require attendance, it simply signals that you need the attendee's input.

- **Optional** These are the people whose attendance is not absolutely necessary for the meeting, but who you think may be interested in attending or participating.

- **Resource** Use this category for the person in charge of the meeting location or any special equipment you need for the meeting (such as a computer or video player).

Follow these steps to select attendees with the Invite button:

1. With Schedule+ open to the Planner view tab, click on the Invite button. (This button is only available if you're using group-enabled mode. See Lesson 1.) See Figure 17.1 to locate the Invite button.

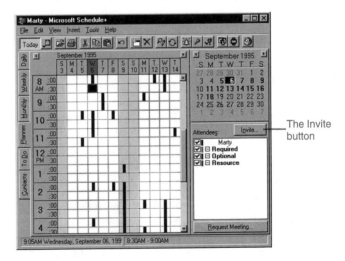

The Invite button

FIGURE 17.1 The Invite button on the Planner view tab.

2. The Select Attendees dialog box appears, as shown in Figure 17.2. You may need to choose another address list from the Show Names from the drop-down list box. Then select the name of a person you want to attend, or type in the name.

Type in a name...

...or select a name that appears in the list box.

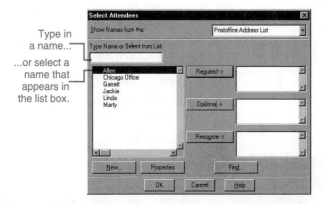

FIGURE 17.2   The Select Attendees dialog box.

3. Next, click on the Required, Optional, or Resource button to assign the attendee to a category.

4. After you choose all of the meeting's participants, click on the OK button to return to the Planner view tab.

TIP   **A Step Ahead**   If you select categories in step 3, you can fill out a Meeting Request form to send out to the attendees more quickly. The names you assign as Required appear in the To line of the request form. The Optional names appear in the Cc line, and the Resource name appears in the Where line. You learn more about the Meeting Request form in Lesson 18.

VIEWING FREE AND BUSY TIMES

There are several ways that you can view the schedules of the attendees. To see the attendees' busy times on the Planner as a group, you should view one attendee category at a time. For example, to see the busy times of the Required attendees, double-click on the Required heading in the Attendees box. A check mark next to the category means that the attendees' schedules appear on the Planner. The busy times for all the attendees in that category appear highlighted by black borders on the Planner grid.

After viewing the busy times, click on the category heading to turn off the display for that category. To view all the attendees in each category, as shown in Figure 17.3, double-click on each heading.

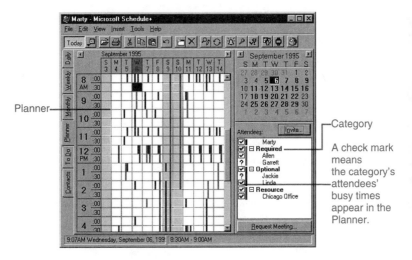

FIGURE 17.3   Use the Attendees box to display the busy times of the people you want to attend your meeting.

Use any of these other methods to change the attendees whose schedules are displayed:

- To view just one user's busy times, double-click on the person's name in the Attendees box. Black borders highlight the person's busy times on the Planner.

- Click anywhere in the Attendeesbox to clear the black borders from the Planner grid.

- To see the names of the people who are busy at a specific time on the Planner, double-click on the time slot or right-click the mouse button.

- To see details about any particular user's schedule, double-click on the busy time slot and select the user's name from the list. If you have access to the user's schedule, you see the details about the user's previously scheduled appointment.

- Click on any time slot on the Planner grid and look over at the Attendees box to see who is busy and who is free. A check mark appears if that person's schedule is in the Planner. A question mark means that person's schedule is not available. An X indicates that the person has a prior commitment during the meeting time.

READING BARS ON A NETWORK PLANNER

As you learned in Lesson 15, the blue bars in your Planner view are exclusive to your schedule. However, when you're networked, you see other colored bars on the Planner as well. When you publish your schedule on the network, it shows other users a colored bar representing the times you are busy. The colored bars help differentiate between users. Depending on what access permissions you assign, other users may or may not be able to see details about your schedule.

Here's how to read the colored bars in your Planner view:

- The gray bars on the Planner indicate the busy times of the required attendees at your meetings.

- The purple bars are busy times for the optional folks attending your meetings.

- The green bars represent busy times for the resource (meeting location or equipment).

Remember, you can double-click on a time block to see details about an attendee's appointments, as long as you have access to the attendee's schedule.

Selecting a Meeting Time

The next step in arranging a meeting is picking out an appropriate time. After you decide who should attend and you view the free and busy times of the attendees, you're ready to select a meeting time.

Probably one of the best tools you can use when you schedule meetings is the AutoPick feature. You can use it to quickly locate free blocks of time for all attendees on the Planner. Here's what you do:

1. Select the time slot (one or more) in which you want to schedule the meeting—try to pick the earliest date or time you need.

2. Now open the Tools menu and select AutoPick. Schedule+ goes to work, locating the earliest time available for all the attendees and highlighting it on the Planner schedule.

3. If you like the time suggested, click on the Request Meeting button and send out your invitations. If you don't like the time suggested, select Tools, AutoPick and do it again until you find a suitable time.

In this lesson, you learned how to prepare for meetings with other users on your network by determining who should attend and selecting a time for the meeting. In the next lesson, you'll learn how to send out Meeting Request forms to invite people to the meeting.

SENDING MEETING REQUESTS ON A NETWORK

18

In this lesson, you will learn how to send out meeting invitations and manage responses to the requests on your network.

CALLING A MEETING

Once you find an appropriate time to have the meeting (see Lesson 17), you're ready to invite the attendees. You need to use the Meeting Request form. Mind you, everybody you invite has to be hooked up to a mail server and the Microsoft Exchange system in order to receive your invitation. (This includes people you're inviting who are outside of your network environment, such as colleagues at other companies.) Although Schedule+ automates scheduling and tracking of meetings, all attendees do not have to have Schedule+ to receive invitations to your meeting. If you meet these requirements, you're ready to start sending out meeting requests—the actual invitations to attend the meeting.

You can use Schedule+'s Meeting Wizard to help you call a meeting. You can also use the Request Meeting button on the Planner tab. When you set up a meeting, you must identify all the people whom you are inviting, choose a meeting time, send out request messages, and receive responses to the messages. First, take a look at the Meeting Request form.

SENDING OUT INVITATIONS WITH THE MEETING REQUEST FORM

To invite the attendees yourself, you can fill out the Meeting Request form and e-mail it to the people you want to attend. Follow these steps to use this feature:

1. From the Planner view tab, click on the Request Meeting button in the Attendees box.

2. The Meeting Request dialog box appears, as shown in Figure 18.1. If you've already determined the names of the people attending and their appropriate categories, you notice that Schedule+ fills in the top portion of the form with this information. If not, you need to fill in the text boxes indicating where you are holding the meeting and who needs to attend (fill in the To and Cc boxes).

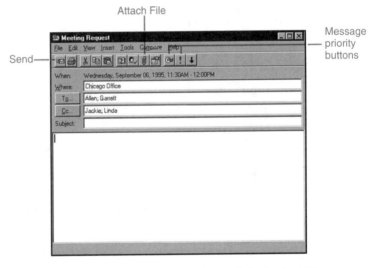

FIGURE 18.1 The Meeting Request form. (It looks just like a typical e-mail form.)

3. Next, click inside the Subject text box and type a description of the meeting. This description appears in the schedules of the attendees.

4. Use the large text box to add any notes about the meeting or to type a meeting memo.

5. If you need to attach files to the message or prioritize message importance, use the toolbar buttons to do so. (You use these same toolbar buttons on the network e-mail system.)

6. When you're ready to send the message, click on the Send button on the toolbar. This sends the e-mail request and exits the form.

USING THE MEETING WIZARD

An easier way to send invitations is with the Meeting Wizard. The Meeting Wizard button appears on your Schedule+ screen if you're using group-enabled mode. Take a look at Figure 18.2 to find the button. To use it, click on the Meeting Wizard button on your toolbar and follow the prompts that appear. The Meeting Wizard leads you through all the steps and coordinates a time and date for the meeting. All you have to do is answer its questions and click on the Next buttons to proceed from dialog box to dialog box. Keep in mind that each wizard dialog box focuses on a particular aspect of the meeting, such as who to invite or where to hold the meeting.

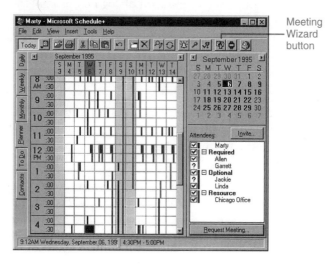

Meeting Wizard button

FIGURE 18.2   The Meeting Wizard button appears on your toolbar if you're using group-enabled mode.

To use the Meeting Wizard, follow these steps:

1. Click on the Meeting Wizard button on the toolbar (see Figure 18.2), or open the Tools menu and select Make Meeting.

2. The Meeting Wizard dialog box appears, as shown in Figure 18.3. Select the categories of people you want to attend and click on the Next button.

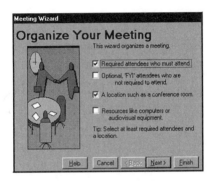

FIGURE 18.3   The first Meeting Wizard dialog box.

3. The second Meeting Wizard dialog box prompts you to select the names of your attendees. You can type the names directly or select them from your network Address Book (click on the Pick Attendees button). After selecting names, click on the Next button to continue to yet another wizard dialog box.

4. The next wizard dialog box gives you the option of selecting a location in which to hold your meeting. Make your selection and click on Next to continue to another wizard dialog box.

5. In the next Meeting Wizard dialog box, you can select a duration time for the meeting. You can even factor in driving time if you are holding the meeting off-site. Make your selections and click on Next.

6. The next wizard dialog box asks you to choose an acceptable time range and potential days for holding your meeting. Make your selections and click on Next.

 Warning! A warning box appears if Schedule+ cannot find information about a requested attendee. This only happens if you choose an attendee who is not using Schedule+ on your network, or if the person isn't using Schedule+ in group-enabled mode.

7. In the next wizard dialog box, you can see the available free and busy times of the attendees you're inviting, and Meeting Wizard enables you to find out which dates, times, and locations are good for all attendees. If you don't like the time the Meeting Wizard chooses, click on the Pick Next Time button to have Meeting Wizard locate another time. Click on Next to continue to another wizard dialog box.

8. When you make it through all of the Meeting Wizard's questions, it prompts you to send a Meeting Request form. Click on the Finish button, and the Meeting Request form appears on-screen (refer to Figure 18.1).

9. The Meeting Request form lists all the attendees whom you want to invite, and the time and location of the meeting. Fill in the rest of the form and click on the Send button on the toolbar to send out the invitations.

TRACKING RESPONSES

As each attendee responds to your meeting request, the responses show up in your Inbox (part of your network e-mail system). You can easily identify the responses by symbols.

You're Invited If you happen to receive an invitation, open it up by double-clicking on the meeting request message; Schedule+ coordinates the request with your schedule and lets you know if you can make it or not. To automatically reply, click on the Accept, Decline, or Tentatively Accept button. This opens a mail window in which you can respond to the originator.

The originator of a meeting request can track responses to the invitations and find out who's coming to the meeting and who's not. If you're the one doing all the inviting, here's how to track the attendees' responses:

1. Open your schedule to the Daily view tab and double-click on the meeting slot in your appointment book to open the Appointment dialog box.

2. Click on the Attendee tab to bring it to the front.

3. As each attendee responds to the request, her name appears in the list with a symbol next to it. The symbol indicates the attendee's status regarding your meeting. Table 18.1 shows what each symbol means.

4. To close the dialog box, click OK

TABLE 18.1   IDENTIFYING RESPONSES TO MEETING INVITATIONS

SYMBOL	MEANING
✓	Accepts invitation
✗	Declines invitation
✓?	Tentatively accepts invitation

SYMBOL	MEANING
	Accepts and includes a message response
	Declines and includes a message response
	Tentatively accepts and includes a message response
	No response yet

> **Need Extra Help?**   To learn more about using Schedule+ in a network environment, have your network administrator give you a few lessons.

In this lesson, you learned how to arrange meetings with other users on your network. In the next lesson, you'll learn how to customize your Schedule+ program.

19 CUSTOMIZING YOUR SCHEDULE

In this lesson, you will learn how to customize your Schedule+ program.

THE OPTIONS DIALOG BOX

You learned a little about customizing your Schedule+ program back in Lesson 4 when you changed the time increments on the Daily view tab and customized the background colors. There are some other ways you can customize the program using the Options dialog box.

To open the Options dialog box, simply pull down the Tools menu and select Options. To close the dialog box at any time without activating your changes to the settings, click on the Cancel button.

The following descriptions tell what each tab in the Options dialog box contains:

The **Defaults** tab contains default settings for appointments, tasks, and contacts.

The **General** tab has options for controlling your workweek's start day, work and non-work hours, and options for using the reminder feature.

The **Display** tab holds settings for controlling the colors and backgrounds of the Schedule+ features.

The **Time Zone** tab enables you to select a time zone for your schedule. (You learned how to change time zones in Lesson 4.)

The **Synchronize** tab enables you to synchronize the schedule on your computer with the schedule you post on the network. This is useful if you use Schedule+ in a network situation.

In the next few sections, you learn how to use the Options dialog box to help you customize your own Schedule+ program.

CHANGING DEFAULT OPTIONS

The Defaults tab holds all your Schedule+ default settings, such as whether the program adds reminders to every appointment you type in on the daily schedule.

Here's a summary of the various settings and what they control:

The **Set reminders for appointments automatically** check box enables you to control whether Schedule+ automatically assigns a reminder icon to any appointment you type into your daily schedule in the Daily view tab. The options directly below the check box enable you to designate the default time setting the program assigns to the reminder and the time increment format (hours, minutes, and so on).

The **Set reminders for tasks automatically** check box enables you to add reminders to any tasks you enter into the To Do list grid in the To Do tab. The options directly below the check box enable you to designate dates regarding the reminders.

The **Default task priority** and the **Default project priority** options enable you to assign priority levels to the tasks and projects you enter into your To Do list grid.

Use the **Default task duration** option to set a default time length in days (or weeks or months) to the tasks you add in the To Do list grid; use the **Default estimated effort** option to set a time span for the tasks.

The **Default business phone** and **Default home phone** settings change the primary phone numbers the program displays in the Contacts list.

Follow these steps to change the default settings:

1. With the Options dialog box open on your screen, click on the Defaults tab to bring it to the front of the dialog box, as shown in Figure 19.1.

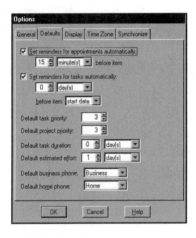

FIGURE 19.1   The Defaults tab.

2. Select the option you want to change, or make changes directly in the settings boxes.

3. Click on the OK button to put the new default settings into effect.

You can always reopen the Options dialog box and the Defaults tab to adjust the settings again later.

SPECIFYING WORKWEEK AND WORKDAY

The General tab in the Options dialog box holds settings that affect when your schedule week starts, which days are work days and non-work days, which hours are work hours and non-work hours, and what time increments Schedule+ displays, among other things. You learned how to change time increments on your schedule in Lesson 4.

The time increment display is rather obvious when you see your schedule, but the designated workdays and work hours may not be so obvious. Take a look at Figure 19.2. Which day your work-week starts on affects the display of days in the Date Navigator calendar and the days of the week in the Weekly view tab. The workdays and hours also have an effect on the background colors of your schedule. The workweek appears in a brighter shade of color on the schedule, and non-work days and hours appear in a darker shade.

The Date Navigator's designated workweek start day

FIGURE 19.2   The subtle differences in color on your schedule represent work days and hours and non-work days and hours.

Not everybody uses the same workdays and work hours, so you can adjust these settings on Schedule+ to help you tailor the pro-gram to your situation. To change the settings for workweeks and workdays, you use the General tab in the Options dialog box.

To change which day of the week your workweek starts on and which work hours you want to focus on, follow these steps:

1. With the Options dialog box open, click on the General tab to bring this tab to the front, as shown in Figure 19.3.

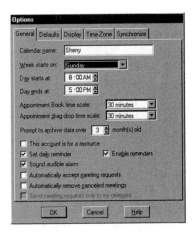

FIGURE 19.3 The General tab in the Options dialog box.

2. To change the day, click on the Week starts on drop-down list arrow and select the appropriate day.

3. To change the hours you designate as your work hours and non-work hours, change the settings in the Day starts at and Day ends at drop-down list boxes.

4. To exit the dialog box and put the settings into effect, click OK.

Also in the General tab are options for changing your schedule's name, controlling how your reminder boxes appear to remind you of an appointment or task, and setting up your schedule as a source account. The following points explain how to use these other General tab options:

• To change the name of your schedule, click on the Calendar name box and type a new name over the existing name.

• Make sure you select the Sound audible alarm and Enable reminders check boxes if you want to be able to hear and see the reminders you assign to appointments and tasks.

- If you're using Schedule+ on a network, you can set up your schedule as a source account by selecting the This account is for a resource check box. This is only necessary if you're in charge of scheduling conference rooms or equipment with your calendar.

CUSTOMIZING TABS

By default, Schedule+ starts out with six tabs to view different features of the program: Daily, Weekly, Monthly, Planner, To Do, and Contacts. However, you can customize the tabs. For instance, if you want to use two Daily view tabs, one showing an enlarged Appointment Book and another showing an enlarged daily To Do list box, you can add another Daily view tab and give it another name.

If you use Schedule+ on a network, the ability to use a tab more than once is especially handy. For example, if you're assigned the role of Delegate Owner and are responsible for tracking your boss's schedule, you need a second set of tabs in Schedule+ to help you manage your boss's schedule as well as your own.

To add a tab to Schedule+, follow these steps:

1. Open the View menu and select Tab Gallery.

2. This opens the Tab Gallery dialog box, shown in Figure 19.4. The list on the left side of the box shows available tabs, and the list on the right shows tabs the program currently displays.

3. Select the tab you want to add from the Available tabs list box. (Click on the name to select it.)

4. Click on the Add button to add the tab to the list on the right.

5. In the Tab title text box, type a new name for the tab.

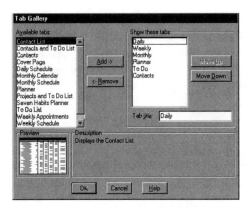

FIGURE 19.4   The Tab Gallery dialog box enables you to add or remove tabs.

6. To rearrange the order of tabs on the list, use the Move Up and Move Down buttons. Click on the tab you want to relocate in the list and click on the appropriate up or down button until the tab's name reaches the correct order in the list.

7. When you finish with the Tab Gallery box, click OK to exit and put your additions into effect.

To remove a tab at any time:

1. Open the Tab Gallery dialog box.

2. Click on the tab you want to remove in the Show these tabs list.

3. Click on the Remove button.

4. Click OK to exit the dialog box.

In this lesson, you learned how to customize different elements of your Schedule+ program. In the next lesson, you'll learn how to import and export schedule data.

IMPORTING AND EXPORTING FILES

In this lesson, you will learn how to export from and import data to your Schedule+ program.

EXPORTING DATA

By now, you know how to compile lists and databases of information, such as task lists and contacts lists. As with most computer programs, you can export your Schedule+ data so that others can use it, or so you can work with it on another computer.

If you're using Schedule+ on a network, you can share your data through e-mail. But what if you're not using Schedule+ on a network, and you need to share information with others? You can easily copy or export your data onto floppy disks or into other locations on your hard drive. You can also convert your data into a format that you can use with other scheduling programs, or you can convert the data into text format. For example, you can export portions of your schedule to use with other scheduling applications, such as Lotus Organizer, PackRat, and ACT! for Windows.

With Schedule+, you can choose to export your entire schedule, your appointments, the To Do list, the Contacts list, and the Events list. You can even designate which dates of your schedule to export.

EXPORTING YOUR DATA ONTO A DISK

When you export your data onto a floppy disk or any other drive or folder on your computer, you need to type a specific path in the Export Schedule+ Interchange dialog box. For example, to export a schedule onto a disk in your A: drive, you type the path statement **A:*schedulename*.SC2** into the File name text box.

The first part of the path indicates which drive you are copying to, and the second part is the name and file extension of your file. All schedule files use the .SC2 file extension.

To export your own data into a Schedule+ file to use with another computer's Schedule+ program, use these steps:

1. Pull down the File menu, select Export, and choose Schedule+ Interchange.

2. The Export Schedule+ Interchange dialog box appears, as shown in Figure 20.1. Type the path and file name to export to into the File name text box.

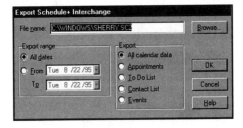

FIGURE 20.1   The Export Schedule+ Interchange dialog box.

3. In the Export area of the dialog box, select the type of data you want to export.

4. In the Export range area of the dialog box, specify which dates you want to export. For example, if you want to export your entire schedule, click on the All dates option. If you only want to export a certain range of dates, specify the range in the From and To boxes.

Exporting Contacts   If you export the Contacts list, the Export range options in the dialog do not apply and appear dimmed.

5. Click OK to exit the dialog box. You see a progress indicator box, similar to Figure 20.2, that tracks the exporting until it's complete.

FIGURE 20.2   The progress indicator box shows you how far along you are in the export process.

EXPORTING DATA AS TEXT

Schedule+ has a helpful Text Export Wizard to assist you with exporting your schedule into a text format file format. When you convert your schedule data into text data, you're taking all the various fields in your database and giving the fields a text structure that resembles a table. Text format is a readily recognized format to many programs, which makes it an ideal format to use when you need data from two distinctly different applications. For example, you can export your Schedule+ data into a Microsoft Word document.

To export a schedule as a text file, follow these steps:

1. Open the File menu, select Export, and select Text.

2. The Text Export Wizard opens on-screen, as shown in Figure 20.3. Select the part of your schedule you want to export and click on the Next button.

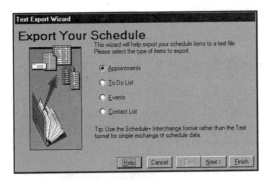

Figure 20.3   The Text Export Wizard.

3. Depending on the data type you select, the Text Export Wizard presents you with a series of dialog boxes that help you determine how the data should conform into a text mode. Choose from the options in the dialog boxes and click on the Next button to continue.

4. One of the dialog boxes you encounter prompts you to decide how the schedule fields appear as text data (see Figure 20.4). By default, the Text Export Wizard separates the fields by commas and surrounds text with quotation marks.

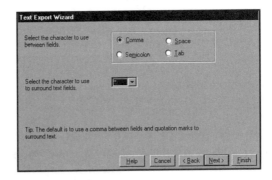

Figure 20.4   This Text Export Wizard dialog box enables you to decide how to display the database in text form.

5. Another dialog box you see (Figure 20.5) enables you to decide exactly which fields to export. Select the fields to export from the Available event fields list and click the Add button. Schedule+ places the fields in the Export Fields list.

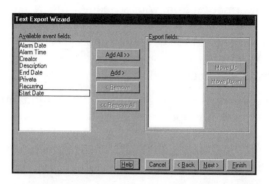

FIGURE 20.5   Choose which fields you want to export from the Available event fields list.

6. The final dialog box, shown in Figure 20.6, prompts you to select a location and name for the data you're exporting. Type the location and name (path) in the File name text box, and click on the Finish button. Schedule + exports your data.

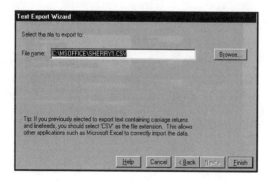

FIGURE 20.6   The final dialog box enables you to determine a location for the exported text.

Exporting to Other Scheduling Systems

Schedule+ can also help you export your data into other scheduling systems, such as other personal information managers (PIMs) or personal digital assistants (PDAs). For example, if you own a Sharp electronic organizer, such as a Sharp Wizard, you can download information from your Schedule+ program onto the pocket computer to take it with you everywhere you go. To follow this export route, open the File menu and select Export, Other Systems. You must select a target system to export to. Then select specific portions of your schedule to export.

To learn more about exporting your schedule information onto specific systems that support Schedule+ data, click on the Help button in the Select Target System dialog box. This opens the Select Systems information in the online help documentation so you can read more about system compatibility and transfer.

Importing Data

Just as you can export your Schedule+ data to other files or computers, you can also import data into your schedule. For example, if you need to coordinate an upcoming seminar with a colleague from another company, you can import your colleague's schedule onto your Schedule+ program. You can import data from other Schedule+ programs, backup schedules, and data from network users' schedules. You can also import schedule information from other scheduling programs such as ACT!, PackRat, and Lotus Organizer.

Something interesting happens when you import appointments into your schedule. Any conflicting time slot assignments appear side by side with your appointments in the Appointment Book.

To import data from another Schedule+ program into your schedule, use these steps:

1. Open the File menu and select Import. In the submenu, choose Schedule+ Interchange.

2. The Import Schedule+ Interchange dialog box appears (see Figure 20.7). In the Look in drop-down list box, select the file or folder you want to import.

FIGURE 20.7 The Import Schedule+ Interchange dialog box.

3. Type the name of the import file in the File name text box, or select the file from the list of files.

4. Click on the Open button to start the importing procedure. A progress indicator marks the completion progress of the task. When the import procedure is complete, your schedule contains the imported data.

IMPORTING DATA AS TEXT

As mentioned earlier in this lesson, not all programs are compatible, and it's not always easy to exchange data. If you import data from a program that doesn't recognize the Schedule+ file format, you may have to convert data into a format with which Schedule+ can work. Text format (TXT file extension) is one of the most common formats you can use. If you import data as text, you use a series of wizard dialog boxes to help you convert the format for use in Schedule+ and choose a location for the data (such as your Appointment Book for appointments, or your To Do list for those tasks).

Follow these steps to use the Text Import Wizard:

1. Open the File menu and select Import , Text . This opens
   the Text Import Wizard dialog box, shown in Figure 20.8.

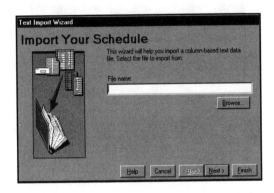

FIGURE 20.8   The first dialog box of the Text Import Wizard.

2. Type the path of the file you're importing, or click on the
   Browse button to locate the file. Click Next to continue to
   another wizard dialog box.

3. In the next wizard dialog box, you can view the first several lines of text in the file. If the first line lists field
   names, select the Yes option. Click on Next to continue.

4. The third wizard dialog box prompts you to select how
   you want to separate the text fields. Select an option and
   click on the Next button.

5. Yet another wizard dialog box appears, this time prompt-
   ing you to choose which data category you want to apply
   to the imported text, such as appointments or Contacts
   list. Select a data and click on Next .

6. The final wizard dialog box enables you to select a type
   for the text fields. Click on the field name, and then select a field category from the drop-down list at the right
   to assign the appropriate field that matches your Sched-
   ule+ format.

7. Click on the Finish button, and Schedule+ converts the
   data into your program.

If you're importing data from a program with a format Schedule+
recognizes, you can use the Other Systems option. This option is
similar to the option for exporting data to other systems. Open
the File menu and select Import, Other Systems You must select a
source system from which to import. Then select a specific data
type in your schedule to which you import the data.

In this lesson, you learned how to import and export Schedule+
data. In the next lesson, you'll learn how to export portions of
your schedule onto a Timex Data Link watch.

LESSON 21

EXPORTING DATA TO THE TIMEX DATA LINK WATCH

In this lesson, you will learn how to export data from your Schedule+ program onto the Timex Data Link watch.

USING SCHEDULE+ WITH A WATCH

If you're the lucky owner of a Timex Data Link watch, you can use it in conjunction with your Schedule+ program. Microsoft and Timex teamed up to create this technologically advanced system that goes wherever you do. By downloading your calendar onto a watch, you don't have to worry about being near your computer to know when your appointments are—you just carry the data on your wrist wherever you go.

The catch to this technology is that you have to own a Timex Data Link watch. Schedule+ doesn't export data onto any other watches.

You can choose to export certain parts of your Schedule+ data, such as appointments, a task list, or phone numbers from a Contacts list, onto the watch. For example, if you copy your Contacts list phone numbers onto the watch, you can access the phone numbers when you're traveling or making sales calls. If you lose your way to an appointment, you can look up the phone number of the person you're supposed to meet at a moment's notice. All you have to do is access the data on your watch. As you can imagine, this technology goes a long way in making you more productive and giving you the information you need when you need it.

COPYING DATA ONTO A TIMEX DATA LINK WATCH

How do you begin to copy your schedule onto a wrist watch? It's easy with the Timex Watch Wizard. This wizard leads you through the process, helping you set up data to copy by asking you questions along the way.

To use the Timex Watch Wizard, follow these steps:

1. Open the File menu and select Export. In the submenu that appears, select Timex Watch. You can also click on the Timex Watch Wizard button on the toolbar, as shown in Figure 21.1.

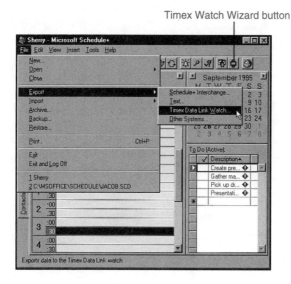

FIGURE 21.1   You access the Timex Watch Wizard from a menu or the toolbar.

2. The Timex Watch Wizard dialog box appears on your screen (see Figure 21.2). Select the data you want to copy onto the watch and click on the Next button.

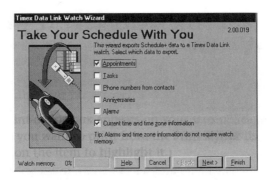

FIGURE 21.2   The Timex Data Watch Wizard dialog box.

3. In the next few dialog boxes, which may vary depending on the data you choose to export, select from the options to designate what dates and data you want to use. Click on the Next button each time you're ready to continue.

4. After you select all the necessary options, you're ready to copy the data onto the watch. Click on the Finish button.

5. The Export to Watch dialog box appears, shown in Figure 21.3. Set your watch to COMM mode with three presses of the green button on the watch. Hold the watch face up to the monitor screen (about two to four inches from the screen) and click the OK button in the dialog box.

6. The monitor screen changes to the Microsoft Transmission mode and starts flashing lines, and the watch beeps as it receives data. The bottom of the screen tells you how far along you are in the transfer process. (Hold your watch steady during the export procedure.)

7. When the export is complete, the monitor screen switches back to the Schedule+ program, and a prompt appears asking you if the export was a success. Click on Yes.

Click here when you're
ready to export.

FIGURE 21.3   When you're ready to copy the data, hold the watch up to the screen and click the OK button in the dialog box.

 Transfer Not Successful?   If the transfer was not successful, you need to clear the watch memory and start all over again. Make sure you follow each step carefully.

Be sure to consult your Timex Data Link watch manual for more information about using the watch and the data you export to it.

In this lesson, you learned how to export Schedule+ data onto a Timex Data Link watch. In the next lesson, you'll learn how to back up and archive data.

22 BACKING UP AND ARCHIVING SCHEDULES

In this lesson, you will learn how to back up and archive your schedules to keep your data safe.

BACK UP YOUR SCHEDULE

In case you haven't noticed by now, Schedule+ doesn't use a traditional way to save data. There's no File, Save command to use every time you exit the program. Instead, Schedule+ saves the data you enter automatically.

Although Schedule+ saves the data automatically, the data isn't always safe. You may have hardware or software complications that result in lost data. For this reason, it's always a smart idea to back up your schedule frequently. In case something ever happens to your current file, you have a copy of all the important appointments, contacts, and tasks saved in the backup file. When you back up your schedule, you're backing up every item in the schedule, including reminders and private data.

You can store your backup file on your hard drive or save it on a floppy disk. By far, the safest way is to store it on a floppy disk. That way, if something happens to your hard drive, you can still access the data.

To back up your schedule, follow these steps:

1. Open the File menu and select Backup.

2. The Select Backup File dialog box appears, as shown in Figure 22.1. From the Save in drop-down list or list box, select a folder or drive in which to back up the file.

FIGURE 22.1   The Select Backup File dialog box.

3. Click inside the File name text box and type a file name
   for the backup. All backup files use a .SCD file extension.
   By default, Schedule+ names the file **BACKUP** (or
   BACKUP.SCD if you're viewing file extensions) unless
   you type another name.

4. Click OK, and Schedule+ copies your entire schedule onto
   the backup file.

RESTORING A BACKUP FILE

Whenever you need the backup copy of your data, you can use
Schedule+'s Restore command to bring it back to your schedule.
The Restore command uses the same password to protect the
backup file that you use to protect your Schedule+ program. You
need to use this password to restore the backup file.

Use these steps to restore a backup file to your Schedule+
program:

1. Open the File menu and select Restore.

2. The Restore Backup File dialog box appears (see Figure
   22.2). Locate the backup file. Use the Look in drop-down
   list box to find the file in other folders or drives. You can
   also type the name of the backup file in the File name
   text box.

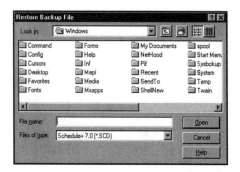

FIGURE 22.2   The Restore Backup File dialog box.

3. Once you locate the file and select it for opening, click on the Open button.

4. The Enter Password dialog box pops up (see Figure 22.3) if you use a password to access Schedule+. Type the password and click OK (The backup file uses the same password as your Schedule+ program.)

FIGURE 22.3   Type your password to restore the file.

5. Next, a warning box appears (see Figure 22.4) telling you that Schedule+ will replace the contents of your schedule with the backup data. Click on Yes to continue, and Schedule+ restores your backup file.

FIGURE 22.4   The restore warning box.

ARCHIVING SCHEDULES

What do you do with the old parts of your schedule that you no longer need to access? With Schedule+, you can archive outdated information. For example, if you no longer need to use the past four months of appointments, you can archive the appointments so you can access the information for reference purposes, but the appointments no longer take up space on your schedule.

By default, Schedule+ prompts you to archive old data every three months. When you archive data, you must specify the dates you want to archive. Schedule+ then stores the data in an archive file.

To archive your data, follow these steps:

1. Open the File menu and select Archive.

2. The Create Archive dialog box appears, as shown in Figure 22.5. Schedule+ assigns a default archive location and file name; however, you can type a new name and location in the File name text box.

FIGURE 22.5   The Create Archive dialog box.

Looking for Another Folder?   If you want to archive the data in another file or folder, click on the Browse button and choose a location for the data from the drives and folders available.

3. To select the dates you want to archive, click on the
   Archive data before drop-down list box to display a calendar from which you can select a date (see Figure 22.6).

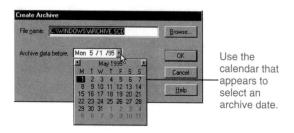

Use the
calendar that
appears to
select an
archive date.

FIGURE 22.6   Select an archive date from the calendar.

4. Click OK, and Schedule+ removes the data from your
   schedule and stores it in the archive file.

Archive files use a .SCD file extension, which means you can open
the archive files like a schedule to view the data at any time.

Archive Reminder   By default, Schedule+ reminds you
to archive every three months, but you can change how
often Schedule+ prompts you to archive. Open the Tools
menu and select Options. Click on the General tab to find
an option for controlling how often Schedule+ reminds
you to archive.

In this lesson, you learned how to back up and archive data. In
the next lesson, you'll learn how to use a special feature called the
Seven Habits of Highly Effective People.

USING THE SEVEN HABITS OF HIGHLY EFFECTIVE PEOPLE

In this lesson, you will learn how to use the Seven Habits of Highly Effective People feature to help you make the most of Schedule+.

WHAT ARE THE SEVEN HABITS OF HIGHLY EFFECTIVE PEOPLE?

Stephen Covey is a best-selling author of business and personal organization books and a leading expert in the field of leadership development. One of his most famous books, *The Seven Habits of Highly Effective People*, explores strategies for helping people prioritize responsibilities and manage a myriad of tasks. These principles are helpful not only in the business field, but also in your personal life.

Covey's book encourages you to develop a personal mission statement to describe what you want to do with your life and define the roles you play in both your work and personal life. Another part of being effective is being able to clearly define goals, both personal and professional. Once you nail down this information, you can begin to put first things first, and achieve greater productivity and fulfillment.

Here are the seven habits you can apply to your own life and personal schedule:

- Be proactive
- Begin with the end in mind
- Put first things first
- Think win-win
- Seek first to understand, then to be understood
- Synergize
- Sharpen the saw

The Seven Habits Tools explain each of these habits in greater detail as you use the tools. Schedule+ incorporates the principles in Covey's book. You can apply the principles by opening the Tools menu and selecting Seven Habits Tools. With the help of several Seven Habits Wizards, you can integrate these habits for effectiveness to your own schedule and practices.

 I Haven't Read the Book! You don't have to read the book in order to use the Seven Habits Tools. You can access a Help menu in the Seven Habits Tools dialog box that contains more information about using these principles in your life and schedule.

Using the Seven Habits Tools

The first step in applying the Seven Habits of Highly Effective People is to open the Seven Habits Tools. The very first time you use the Seven Habits tools, Schedule+ prompts you to use the Overall Wizard for an orientation to the Seven Habits philosophy.

After you work your way through the first wizard series, Schedule+ prompts you to go through three more wizard series to assemble a personal mission statement, establish your daily roles, and develop personal goals. In each wizard series, you walk through each step to define your goals and responsibilities. Answer the questions to the best of your ability. You can always go back and change your answers by opening the wizard series again.

If you are using the Seven Habits Tools for the first time, use these steps to guide you:

1. Pull down the Tools menu and select Seven Habits Tools.

2. This opens the Seven Habits Wizard dialog box, shown in Figure 23.1. (The first time you use this tool, the Wizard feature opens automatically. If the Wizard dialog box does not appear, click on the Wizard button in the Seven Habits Tools window to open the feature.) Select the Overall Wizard option and click on the Next button.

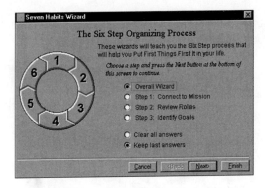

FIGURE 23.1   The Seven Habits Wizard dialog box.

3. The Overall Wizard leads you through a series of dialog boxes. Some dialog boxes contain informational material to read; others contain questions that you can answer to set up your own Seven Habits (see Figure 23.2). Click on the Next button in each dialog box to progress through the series.

4. The final Overall Wizard dialog box prompts you to continue with the other wizards by clicking on the Finish button.

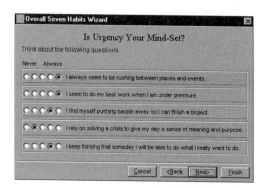

FIGURE 23.2 As you progress through the Overall Wizard's dialog boxes, you encounter some that require you to answer questions.

5. Select the next wizard series to go through and click on the Next button.

6. Again, a wizard leads you through a series of different dialog boxes with questions to answer, as shown in Figure 23.3. Keep clicking on the Next button to continue.

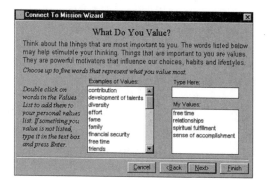

FIGURE 23.3 In each wizard series, you find questions that help you set up your own seven habits.

7. When you finish going through each of the wizard series, click on the Finish button. The Seven Habits Tools dialog box appears (see Figure 23.4) with four tabs containing the information you entered in the dialog boxes.

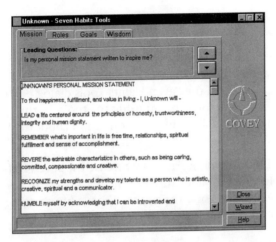

FIGURE 23.4   After you complete each of the wizards, the Seven Habits Tools dialog box appears on-screen.

Here's a description of each tab in the Seven Habits Tools dialog box:

Mission   Use this tab to view and edit your personal mission statement.

Roles   View and edit the important roles in your life and evaluate how effective you are.

Goals   Use this tab to plan activities that correspond to your goals and ideas.

Wisdom   Access documentation to help encourage and enlighten your personal management system and ideas.

8. To reopen any of the Seven Habits wizards, click on the Wizard button in the bottom right corner. To close the Seven Habits Tools box and return to the Schedule+ screen, click on the Close button.

Keep in mind that each person uses the Seven Habits Tools in a different way.

You can read more about using each of the tabs and the Seven Habits by accessing the Seven Habits documentation. Click on the Help button while in the Seven Habits Tools dialog box to display a large list of topics focusing on using the tools. In the Help documentation, you find all kinds of information about the Seven Habits principles and what they can do for you.

In this last lesson, you learned how to use the Seven Habits of Highly Effective People feature of Schedule+. Now that you know the ins and outs of using the program, have fun creating your own schedules.

WINDOWS 95 PRIMER

Microsoft Windows 95 is a graphical operating system that makes your computer easy to use by providing menus and pictures to select. Before you can take advantage of it, however, you must learn some Windows 95 basics.

A FIRST LOOK AT WINDOWS 95

You don't have to start Windows 95—it starts automatically when you turn on your PC. After the initial startup screens, you arrive at a screen something like the one shown in Figure A.1. (Notice how the open programs look on the taskbar in Figure A.1.)

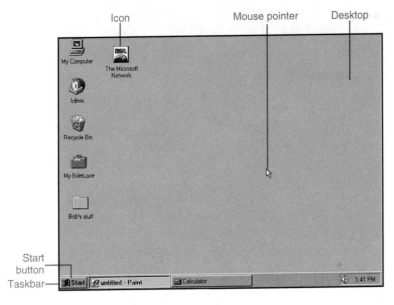

FIGURE A.1 The Windows 95 screen.

Parts of the Screen

As shown in Figure A.1, the Windows 95 screen contains many special elements and controls. Here's a brief summary:

- The background on which all the pictures and boxes rest is the *desktop*.

- The *taskbar* shows the windows and programs that are open. You can switch between open windows and programs by clicking the name on the taskbar.

- The *Start button* opens a menu system from which you can start programs. Click on the Start button; then click on your selection from each menu that appears.

- Some *icons* appear on your desktop. You can activate one by double-clicking on it.

You'll learn more about these elements as we continue.

Also Appearing...   If your computer has Microsoft Office installed on it, you see the Office Shortcuts toolbar on-screen too. It's a series of little pictures strung together horizontally, representing Office programs. Hold the mouse over a picture to see what it does; click on it to launch the program. See your Microsoft Office documentation to learn more.

Using a Mouse

To work most efficiently in Windows, you need a mouse. Here are the mouse actions you need to know:

- *Point* means to move the mouse pointer onto the specified item by moving the mouse. The tip of the mouse pointer must touch the item.

- *Click* on an item means to move the pointer onto the specified item and press and release the mouse button once. Unless you're specifically told to right-click, you click with the left mouse button. Clicking usually selects an item.

- *Double-click* on an item means to move the pointer to the specified item and press and release the left mouse button twice quickly. Double-clicking usually activates an item.

- *Drag* means to move the mouse pointer onto the item, hold down the mouse button, and move the mouse while holding down the button. Unless you're specifically told to right-drag, use the left mouse button.

CONTROLLING A WINDOW WITH THE MOUSE

Windows are the heart of the Windows 95 program. Windows 95 sections off these rectangular areas for particular purposes, such as running a program. You can control a window using the procedures shown in Figure A.2.

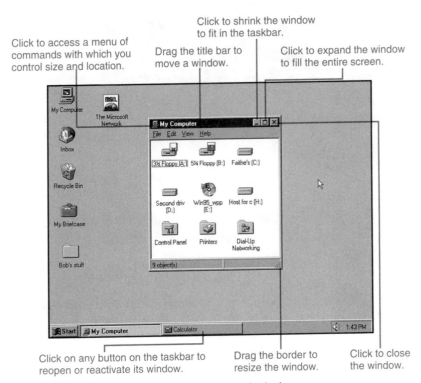

FIGURE A.2   Use your mouse to control windows.

Scroll Bars   If your window contains more icons than it can display at once, scroll bars appear on the bottom and/or right edges of the window. To move through the window's contents, click on an arrow button at either end of a scroll bar to move in that direction, or drag the gray bar in the direction you want to move.

Getting Help

Windows 95 comes with a great online Help system. To access it, click your mouse on the Start button and click on Help. You see the dialog box shown in Figure A.3.

Figure A.3   Windows offers several kinds of help.

There are three tabs in this box: Contents, Index, and Find. The Contents tab appears on top first. To move to another tab, click on it. Here's how to use each tab:

- Contents   Double-click on any book to open it. Sub-books and documents appear. Double-click on sub-books and documents to open them.

- Index   Type the word you want to look up. The Index list scrolls to that part of the alphabetical listing. When you see the topic that you want to read, double-click on it.

- Find   The first time you click on this tab, Windows tells you it needs to create a list. Click Next and Finish to allow this. Then you see the main Find tab. Type the word you want to find in the top text box. Then click a word in the middle box to narrow the search. Finally, review the list of Help topics at the bottom, and double-click the one you want to read.

When you're done reading about a document, click Help Topics to return to the main Help screen, click Back to return to the previous Help topic, or click the window's Close button to exit Help.

STARTING A PROGRAM

There are many ways to start a program, but here is the simplest (see Figure A.4):

1. Click the Start button.

2. Click Programs.

3. Click on the group that contains the program you want to start (for instance, Microsoft Office 95).

4. Click on the program you want to start (for instance, Microsoft Access).

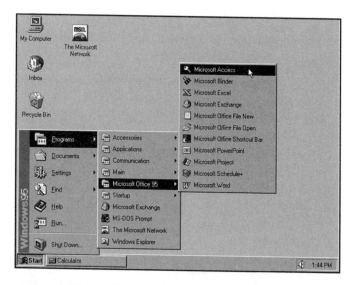

Figure A.4   Click on the Start button; then click on each menu and submenu until you find the program you want to start.

Another way to start a program is to open a document that you created in that program (the program automatically opens when the document opens). Double-click on a document file in My Computer or Windows Explorer to open it, or click the Start button and select a recently used document from the Documents menu.

You can also start a program by double-clicking on its shortcut icon on the desktop. Shortcut icons are links to other files. When you use a shortcut, Windows simply follows the link back to the original file.

Whenever you use a document or program frequently, you might consider creating a shortcut for it on the desktop. To do so, just use the right mouse button to drag an object out of Windows Explorer or My Computer. On the shortcut menu that appears, select Create Shortcut(s) Here.

USING MENUS

Almost all Windows programs have menu bars containing menus. The menu names appear across the top of the screen in a row. To open a menu, click on its name. The menu drops down, displaying its commands (see Figure A.5). To select a command, click on it.

Shortcut Keys Notice in Figure A.5 that key names, such as Enter for the Open command or F8 for the Copy command, appear after some command names. These are shortcut keys. You use these keys to perform the commands without opening the menu.

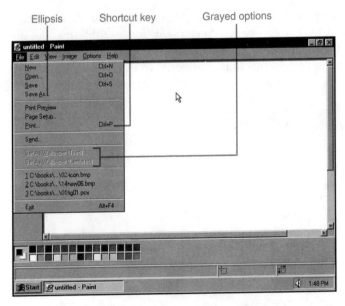

FIGURE A.5 A menu lists various commands you can perform.

Usually, when you select a command, Windows 95 executes the command immediately. However, the following exceptions are true:

- If the command name is gray (instead of black), the command is unavailable at the moment and you cannot choose it.

- If the command name is followed by an arrow, as with the Start button's menus, selecting the command causes another menu to appear, from which you must make another selection.

- If the command is followed by an ellipsis (three dots), selecting it will cause a dialog box to appear. You'll learn about dialog boxes later in this lesson.

Using Shortcut Menus

A new feature in Windows 95 is the shortcut menu. Right-click on any object (any icon, screen element, file, or folder), and a shortcut menu appears, as shown in Figure A.6. The shortcut menu contains commands that apply only to the selected object. Click on any command to select it, or click outside the menu to cancel.

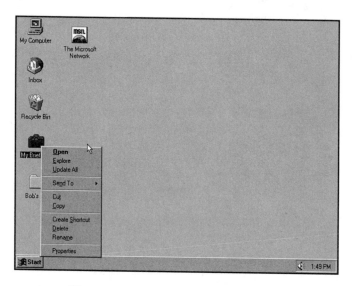

Figure A.6   Shortcut menus are new for Windows 95.

NAVIGATING DIALOG BOXES

A dialog box is the program's way of requesting additional information. For example, if you choose Print from the File menu of the WordPad application, you see a dialog box something like the one shown in Figure A.7. (Its exact look will vary depending on your printer.)

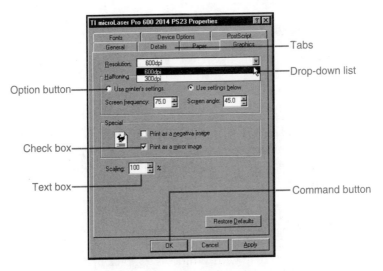

FIGURE A.7   A dialog box requests additional information.

Each dialog box contains one or more of the following elements:

- *Tabs* bring up additional "pages" of options you can choose. Click on a tab to activate it.

- *List boxes* display available choices. Click on any item on the list to select it. If the entire list is not visible, use the scroll bar to find additional choices.

- *Drop-down lists* are similar to list boxes, but only one item in the list is shown. To see the rest of the list, click the down arrow to the right of the list box. Then click on an item to select it.

- *Text boxes* enable you to type in an entry. Just click inside the text box and type. Text boxes that expect numeric input usually have up and down arrow buttons (increment buttons) that let you bump the number up and down.

- *Check boxes* enable you to turn on or off an individual option. Click on a check box to turn it on or off. Each check box is an independent unit that doesn't affect other check boxes.

- *Option buttons* are like check boxes, except option buttons appear in groups, and you can select only one. When you select an option button, Schedule+ deselects any others you already selected. Click on a button to activate it.

- *Command buttons* perform an action, such as executing the options you set, closing the dialog box, or opening another dialog box. To select a command button, click on it.

From Here...

If you need more help with Windows 95, pick up one of these books:

The Complete Idiot's Guide to Windows 95 by Paul McFedries

Windows 95 Cheat Sheet by Joe Kraynak

The Big Basics Book of Windows 95 by Shelley O'Hara, Jennifer Fulton, and Ed Guilford

INDEX

tasks, 70
  categories, 71
  grid display, changing, 71-72
  Contacts list, 102-103
  deleting, 13, 85
  displaying with related project, 82-83
  editing, 84-87
  entering, 76-77
    as appointments, 85
    as projects, 79-83
  grouping, 83-84
  hiding, 83
  printing, 108
  private icon, 13
  selecting, 8
  reminders, 13, 86-87
  shortcuts, 12
  tracking, 87-88
tentative appointments, 46, 109
Tentative button, 13
text
  exporting files as, 151-153
  importing files as, 155-157
Text Export Wizard, 151
Text Export Wizard dialog box, 152
Text Import Wizard, 156
time entries, current, 9
Timex Data Link watch
  COMM mode, 160
  files, exporting to, 158-161
  Microsoft Transmission mode, 160
  uploading schedule to, 13
Timex Watch Wizard, 159
Timex Watch Wizard button, 13
Timex Watch Wizard dialog box, 159
title bar, 8
To Do list, 7, 9, 11, 25, 70
  cells, 75
  editing
    categories, 72-74
    column headings, 85
  grid
    editing display, 71-72
    inserting new row on, 85
    reading grid, 74-75

printing, 108
projects, grouping with tasks, 83-83
rows and columns, 75
tasks
  adding, 76-77
  categories, 71
  editing, 84-87
  grouping with projects, 83-84
  reminders, 86-87
  tracking, 87-88
To Do tab, 11
Today button, 12
toolbar buttons, 8, 12
  Copy, 12, 53
  Cut, 12, 53
  Delete, 13, 48, 95
  Edit, 50, 54, 67
  function, 14
  Go To Date, 12, 115
  Insert New Appointment, 13, 35, 41, 48, 67
  Insert New Contact, 93
  Insert New Task, 76
  Meeting Wizard, 13, 137
  Open, 12
  Paste, 12, 53
  Print, 12, 109
  Private, 13, 45
  Recurring, 13, 44
  Reminder, 13
  Select Today, 12
  Tentative, 13
  Timex Watch Wizard, 13
  Today, 115
  ToolTips, 14
  Undo, 13
  View Mail, 13
Tools menu, 6, 14, 28-30, 42, 44, 65, 71, 121, 123, 125, 134, 138, 142
ToolTips, 14
tracking
  meeting responses, 139-141
  tasks, 87-88
.TXT file extension, importing files as text, 155

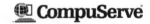

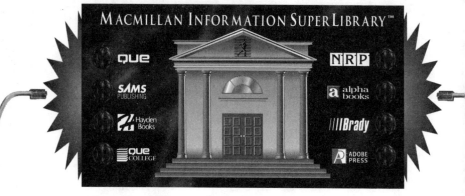

Complete and Return this Card
for a *FREE* Computer Book Catalog

Thank you for purchasing this book! You have purchased a superior computer book written expressly for your needs. To continue to provide the kind of up-to-date, pertinent coverage you've come to expect from us, we need to hear from you. Please take a minute to complete and return this self-addressed, postage-paid form. In return, we'll send you a free catalog of all our computer books on topics ranging from word processing to programming and the internet.

Mr. ☐   Mrs. ☐   Ms. ☐   Dr. ☐

Name (first) ☐☐☐☐☐☐☐☐☐ (M.I.) ☐ (last) ☐☐☐☐☐☐☐☐☐☐☐☐☐☐

Address ☐☐☐☐☐☐☐☐☐☐☐☐☐☐☐☐☐☐☐☐☐☐☐☐

☐☐☐☐☐☐☐☐☐☐☐☐☐☐☐☐☐☐☐☐☐☐☐☐

City ☐☐☐☐☐☐☐☐☐☐ State ☐☐   Zip ☐☐☐☐☐ ☐☐☐☐

Phone ☐☐☐ ☐☐☐ ☐☐☐☐   Fax ☐☐☐ ☐☐☐ ☐☐☐☐

Company Name ☐☐☐☐☐☐☐☐☐☐☐☐☐☐☐☐☐☐☐☐☐☐

E-mail address ☐☐☐☐☐☐☐☐☐☐☐☐☐☐☐☐☐☐☐☐☐☐☐

1. Please check at least (3) influencing factors for purchasing this book.

Front or back cover information on book .... ☐
Special approach to the content .... ☐
Completeness of content .... ☐
Author's reputation .... ☐
Publisher's reputation .... ☐
Book cover design or layout .... ☐
Index or table of contents of book .... ☐
Price of book .... ☐
Special effects, graphics, illustrations .... ☐
Other (Please specify): _____ ☐

2. How did you first learn about this book?

Internet Site .... ☐
Saw in Macmillan Computer
  Publishing catalog .... ☐
Recommended by store personnel .... ☐
Saw the book on bookshelf at store .... ☐
Recommended by a friend .... ☐
Received advertisement in the mail .... ☐
Saw an advertisement in: _____ ☐
Read book review in: _____ ☐
Other (Please specify): _____ ☐

3. How many computer books have you purchased in the last six months?

This book only .... ☐   3 to 5 books .... ☐
2 books .... ☐   More than 5 .... ☐

4. Where did you purchase this book?

Bookstore .... ☐
Computer Store .... ☐
Consumer Electronics Store .... ☐
Department Store .... ☐
Office Club .... ☐
Warehouse Club .... ☐
Mail Order .... ☐
Direct from Publisher .... ☐
Internet site .... ☐
Other (Please specify): _____ ☐

5. How long have you been using a computer?

Less than 6 months .. ☐   6 months to a year ..... ☐
1 to 3 years .... ☐   More than 3 years ...... ☐

6. What is your level of experience with personal computers and with the subject of this book?

	With PC's	With subject of book
New	☐	☐
Casual	☐	☐
Accomplished	☐	☐
Expert	☐	☐

Source Code — ISBN: 0-7897-0568-0

7. Which of the following best describes your job title?

Administrative Assistant .... ☐
Coordinator .... ☐
Manager/Supervisor .... ☐
Director .... ☐
Vice President .... ☐
President/CEO/COO .... ☐
Lawyer/Doctor/Medical Professional .... ☐
Teacher/Educator/Trainer .... ☐
Engineer/Technician .... ☐
Consultant .... ☐
Not employed/Student/Retired .... ☐
Other (Please specify): .... ☐

8. Which of the following best describes the area of the company your job title falls under?

Accounting .... ☐
Engineering .... ☐
Manufacturing .... ☐
Marketing .... ☐
Operations .... ☐
Sales .... ☐
Other (Please specify): .... ☐

9. What is your age?

Under 20 .... ☐
21-29 .... ☐
30-39 .... ☐
40-49 .... ☐
50-59 .... ☐
60-over .... ☐

10. Are you:

Male .... ☐
Female .... ☐

11. Which computer publications do you read regularly? (Please list)

_____
_____
_____
_____
_____
_____
_____
_____
_____
_____

Comments: _____
_____
_____

Fold here and scotch-tape to m

‖·‖·‖·‖·‖·‖·‖··‖·‖·‖·‖··‖‖·‖··‖·‖·‖